Signs of a Soulmate
ASTROLOGY CLUES OF HAPPILY EVER AFTERS

ANMARIE UBER

Also by Anmarie Uber

60 Second Tarot

'Fool' Proof Tarot

5 Numbers of Destiny

Synchronicity Numbers

The Chaldean Numbers System

Number Code

Breaking Your Magnetic Patterns

Recreate Your Identity

Soulmate Poetry

Cheatsheet: How to Name Your Business

My Chaldean Days

Contents

Introduction - Born Weird, Always Weird   xi

1. WHO IS MY SOULMATE?   1
   Signs of a Soulmate   2
   Happily-Ever-After or Hell to Pay?   4

2. PIE IN THE SKY   7
   What is a Natal Chart?   8
   Zodiac Soup   8
   What, Where & How?   9
   What's Your Sign?   13
   Creating Your Zodiac Chart   15
   Putting the Puzzle Together   19
   More Squiggles   22
   Aspects   24

3. THE 12 SIGNS OF VALENTINES   27
   The Roles We Play   28
   Romancing the Signs   31
   Aries   31
   Taurus   39
   Gemini   45
   Cancer   53
   Leo   61
   Virgo   68
   Libra   77
   Scorpio   86
   Sagittarius   95
   Capricorn   102
   Aquarius   111
   Pisces   120

4. ELEMENTS & QUALITIES ... 129
   Four Zodiac Sign Elements ... 129
   What's Your Mode-us Operandi? ... 135
   Ruling Planets ... 139
   Who Rules the Roost? ... 140

5. ASTROLOGY SOULMATE PLACEMENTS ... 143
6. SUN SIGN LINKS ... 147
7. BEST FRIENDS FOREVER ... 157
   Same Sign Friendship Bond ... 158
   Opposite Sign Friendship Bond ... 159
   Sharing each other's House Bond ... 159
   Degrees of Separation or Friendship ... 160

8. HOT AND STEAMY LINKS ... 163
   Sexual Same Sign Bond ... 165
   Sexual Opposite Sign Bond ... 166
   Let's go to my House Bond ... 166
   Degrees of Heat Bond ... 166
   Twin Flame Connections? ... 166

9. THE QUIZ ... 171
   The Soulmate Connection Quiz ... 171

10. REAL LIFE SOULMATES ... 187

11. WRITTEN IN THE STARS - FAMOUS COUPLES ... 201
    A Celebrity Couple with No Known Birth Time ... 219

Afterword ... 223
Appendix ... 225
Notes ... 227
About the Author ... 229

Copyright © 2022 by Anmarie Uber.

All rights reserved.

No part of this publication may be reproduced, distributed or transmitted in any form or by any means, including photocopying, recording, or other electronic or mechanical methods, without the prior written permission of the publisher, except in the case of brief quotations embodied in critical reviews and certain other noncommercial uses permitted by copyright law. For permission requests, write to the publisher, addressed "Attention: Permissions Coordinator," at the address below.

Tuggle Publishing

tugglepublishing.com

anmarieuber.com

Signs of a Soulmate/Anmarie Uber —1st ed.

Quotes taken from "Soulmate Poetry" by Anmarie Uber

 Created with Vellum

Dedicated to: Caroline, Alina, Reinhard, Karen from Cali, Kathy Minnich and all the other Patreons making this book possible. And for Rosella who left behind a book on astrology all those years ago that ended up in my hands.

Introduction - Born Weird, Always Weird

All my life I have been attracted to things outside of the "norm". My desire to learn astrology was not a mainstream interest back in the day. And it was certainly not normal for a child of eight to be desiring this knowledge with no known provocation from the outside world. Much less having any inner intuitive inclinations. At that time, astrology was still considered "weird" or even laughed at – with plenty of people ready to give opinions and debunk it without having studied the system. Most had no clue there was anything more to it than what they read in the newspaper – a generalized daily prediction for each sign. Astrology became an amusement, like reading your fortune cookie. Something fun but not to be taken seriously. In fact, what appeared to be an ancient and well-respected science had been relegated to the masses as a modern joke. But I didn't know any of that at eight years old, and it wouldn't have stopped me from wanting to learn more. Not much did, once I had my mind set on something.

And at that ripe old age of eight I discovered a way to get myself to the mall – a.k.a. - to the bookstore. I would get on the public transportation bus and head to the shopping complex...by myself. And yes, you did read that correctly. In those days, the neighbor kids and I ran around the neighborhood all day unsupervised. When I wasn't in school, I was often outside, only returning home for lunch, and again later when I heard my dad's whistle for dinner. And even after dinner heading back outside until it was close to bedtime. The neighbor kids and I would play "ghost in the graveyard", which was like a hide-and-seek game in the dark. Different times back then.

Anyway, the child me stepped off the bus and entered paradise - the mall - where you could get an Orange Julius, hot pretzels, and of course my ultimate destination, Walden Books. Upon entering I would skim the kid's books and then go right to the alternative section, which was very small and always hidden at the back of the store. My choice of subjects was limited to U.F.O.s, astrology, ghost hauntings and people born with "strange" anomalies. Like someone being able to add extremely large sums in their head within seconds. Or children who could recount details of a past life as someone else. I eagerly perused the titles like it was my birthday. Books made me feel that way. And because of them I had access to astrology, which would become a lifelong study. Eventually I bought Whitley Streiber's books "Communion" and "Transformation" on gray ET abductions in high school. My choice in reading material disturbed my mother and she would often go through my room, confiscating books that I "shouldn't be reading". I never did drugs, but instead got in trouble for my book addiction.

But back to astrology - I was drawn to the stars because they represented a place that wasn't here. Somewhere that felt like home. Laying out on the middle of our frozen pond at night, with an encyclopedia stuck under my arm and a red light to read with. I learned to identify the different constellations. After naming off a few, my mother got the idea that I should be an astronomer. So, I looked into a total of one astronomy book, Carl Sagan's "Cosmos" (a Scorpio by the way), and the part that stuck with me was his belief that it would be ignorant to believe aliens did *not* exist. What also stuck with me was I knew I didn't want to be an astronomer – *boring*! I intuitively knew there was something more to life than what mainstream science or media was telling me. When I discovered astrology, it was if a doorway had opened to those bright dots in the sky. There was meaning to them being there. There was a method and pattern to the Universe, and we were included in that grand equation of moving parts.

Astrology originally became a way for me to understand myself and to anticipate behaviors from others. It actually made me a more compassionate and understanding person with people who would normally irritate or frustrate me. I could see their pattern or overlay/archetype playing out through their personality – and suddenly it was okay for them to think or be different than I was. To be their own expression. And I could learn to love them better. Which meant I could be me and love me too. But I was always hoping for more – I needed answers to the "big" questions answered of "Who am I?", "Where did I come from?", and "How did I get here?" But that is a story for another day. Astrology helped understand me and why I felt I didn't fit into this world (besides being an extreme introvert), and why was I so different from my extroverted "non-weird" family. Insecurities set in when we moved, and I changed schools in 5th grade. Whatever false sense of my highly-functioning extrovert self that I still held onto, became even harder to prop up with a bully at school vying for control. I was used to being thrust in a leadership role at my old school – the popular girl that everyone followed. A role I did not want but found myself in, nonetheless. At the new school I withdrew into myself even more. But I never stopped studying people through the different lenses of the zodiac, attempting to understand.

In my teen years, I became more interested in the romance aspect of astrology, but it was still a hard thing to pin down – that elusive link that created compatibility? That sign you were "supposed" to click with didn't match up so perfectly in real life. Which drove me to start testing things. I needed more information than what the books were giving me.

At twenty-one I began hand drawing basic charts (before astrology computer programs became widely available). I kept them simple for a few reasons, one being that the math required was very involved. But I found that I could still attain a high degree of accuracy using the basics of a chart. And of course, I did what most do when they are interested in something, I began to *talk* about astrology. Before long, people were requesting charts to understand themselves better and their relationships. What I learned was that most people are lost and faking their way through life, as well as through love. Lacking an understanding of their own nature and impact on the world around them and running programs of how they were supposed to act or giving reactive responses.

In all my studies of astrology I think what interested me most were those very things – what makes us tick and how we match up romantically with someone else. I began to narrow my focus and attention on romance, compatibility and long-term relationships. I knew a lot of people stayed together due to religious beliefs, or not wanting to break up a family. Some stayed together for the sake of public image or financial security. And many relationships fractured due to character flaws and outside influences that broke down the initial attraction. I was driven to find the key astrology markers that were shared between couples who stayed together. Those that possibly had strong foundations in previous lifetimes that added to a solid connection in this life. What were the patterns in an astrology chart that signaled you were with one of *these* people?

Over time the similarities began to show themselves. And the more of these placements you had, the more likely you were to stay together. Couples with certain astrology criteria shared an attraction for each other that never faded, or they ended up best of friends. There was often a feeling of "having known each other before".

The relationships that started out strong, but fell apart, lacked these astrology connections. Possibly there were too many character differences between them in important and basic ways. Or they were together for the wrong reasons without enough glue to get them through the tough times. But when you make an attempt to become emotionally healthy and try to understand where others are coming from, the chances of relationship success and longevity have a much greater chance of becoming a reality, even with challenging astrology charts. But many enter a relationship focusing on what they will "get" instead of what they can "give". A give and take must be present with both parties for harmony and long-term love. And that does not mean overcompensating for a partner's lack of effort. Or staying in something long past the due date. Or worse, allowing a partner to abuse you. I saw a meme that said, "Unconditional love is not unconditional tolerance." So, isn't it time to search for someone that you can make happy, and can give back to you as well? Someone you can depend on, who has your back and tries to understand your needs?

After years of compiling this data on couples, I asked myself, "How can I break this all down into a simple roadmap that anyone could follow, without knowing anything about astrology?" I wanted a system that could quickly analyze whether a partnership is one that could last. For both readers that wanted to take a toe dip into astrology and for those desiring to study at length. And so, this book was born. It has been waiting to be written for about the last fifteen years. As more people are becoming interested in astrology, I decided not to wait any longer. Let's get to this! Does that special someone you have your eye on have potential to turn into lasting love? Let's find out...

Enjoy!
Much Love,
Anmarie

P.S. This book is based on western Tropical astrology. If you would like your astrology chart(s) analyzed by me, please go to my website at anmarieuber.com/services.

CHAPTER 1
Who is My Soulmate?

Many of us find ourselves on the rocky road of relationships that lead to eating a pint of Rocky Road ice cream. The stats always seem to be against us finding true love. The "love is blind" blindfold gets ripped off our starry eyes and we discover the truckload of baggage - hang-ups, issues and conflicts - buried underneath that dreamy smile. We begin to ask ourselves why it seemed so right at first, yet everything went so wrong. Why does only a small percentage of people find the love of their life and go on to celebrate decades of anniversaries?

I think a big part of the answer lies in having shared past-life experiences. When you have had a past life together, it creates a bond or a connection that is recognizable on some unconscious level the next time you meet. And based on those earlier experiences you can bet that individual is coming back into your life to do one of two things: Either to make you "pay" for what happened previously between the two of you or to be a blessing/reward. These people that you have known in other lifetimes are what I call "soulmates" and bring either intensely difficult or intensely wonderful experiences. They are the heavy-hitters. The ones who pull on your heartstrings, maybe literally by ripping your heart out, or with treasured memories. Our soul never forgets them. So - hint-hint - we are looking for the blessing/reward soulmates who protected our hearts and treated us well.

SIGNS OF A SOULMATE

When you have had previous lives with an individual, you will feel a sense of recognition. You may have thoughts about them, such as "I have known this person before," or "I feel so comfortable and safe with them," or "They complete me." That feeling of having known someone or believing they are your other half is the hallmark of past-life soulmates. These types of relationships stand out from the average. The magnetic draw seems inescapable. And the result of getting involved is a crapshoot for happiness. Either you get a sucker punch to the gut, a ride on the rainbow to happily ever after or a combo of both – when the rainbow ends with a sucker punch. What makes it good or bad in terms of experience is the "karma" between the two of you. Meaning whatever went on in the past life will usually carry over into this one. Were you happy together and treated each other well? Great, you may have an opportunity to be happy again. Was the relationship difficult, or did one of you abuse the other? If so, you might be cycling back through another karmic pattern together, so buckle up. But how do you tell which it is? I believe astrology can provide that information, but I will get to that in a bit. Let's talk about karma first.

According to the dictionary, kismet or karma is "a pre-determined or unavoidable destiny". I think the definition is wrong, and I'll tell you why. It is describing cause and effect, not karma. "Karma is going to get you!" is a statement people love to toss around. As if the universe or some higher power is keeping tally and will take care of punishing someone who has stolen your bicycle. I understand some religions believe this, but I don't think in those terms. Let's break it down. A statement like "I have good karma coming to me" suggests that you will be rewarded for doing good in the world. This may or may not happen because as I suggested, I don't believe higher laws operate on reward and punishment for past deeds. They operate on "cause and effect". There is a big difference between cause-and-effect and karmic payment-reward cycles. Cause and effect teaches you about the world. If you do "A" you get "B". An example of cause and effect is staying out in the Sun too long which could cause you to either get burned or suffer heat stroke. By this experience you learn to understand how the Sun works and make sure that next time you are catching a few rays you monitor the time you spend outside. The Sun does *not* however operate on reward and punishment. It will send the same amount of sunshine, regardless of whether a person is good or bad. Reward and punishment, therefore, are *human beliefs and choices*. To reward means to thank someone by choosing to give a happy experience to them, and to punish is to make someone pay - usually based on vengeance/anger etc. Or turning it on yourself, believing you should be punished which is based on shame or guilt.

Another example: If you plant an apple tree and give it what it needs (sunlight, trimming, nutrients) it will grow apples. The apple tree operates with Universal Law – if you do "A" (give it nutrients and care) you will get "B" (apples). If you decide to share the apples with people you like, this is reward. When you do not share them with people who want them, this is called punishment. You are choosing their reward or punishment, depending. The apple tree itself does not choose who gets the apples and who does not. It simply grows them and gives to whomever chooses to reach up and pick. So basic life does not work according to reward and punishment, but rather cause and effect. Rewarding and punishing are human inventions.

When it comes to past lives, I think we chose to have reward karma in this life for whatever we did well, and payment karma for what we did poorly or failed to do at all. Another person may want to incarnate with you to reward or punish you as well, based on kindnesses or crimes you did to them in the past. They find you in this lifetime to mete out your due. And you agree to the meetup – because you think you deserve to suffer for it, or you want to make amends and even the scales of perceived justice. Both souls agree to these punishment and reward cycles for various reasons. We incarnate back in and allow these cycles to happen due to guilt for actions we want to rectify, or we want to reward ourselves for our good deeds. It is a combination of our agreement to suffer or get rewarded in this life with other souls. But we can always say "no". Which means *we do not have to play out our karma in our personal lives or with another person if we do not want to – we can make a different choice.* There is almost always a choice.

I have written books on how to cancel out karma, but this particular book is about recognizing whether a partner or prospective partner is a soulmate who brings "good karma" - the possibility of a rewarding and lasting relationship.

HAPPILY-EVER-AFTER OR HELL TO PAY?

So, how do you know if a current or potential partner will be a royal pain in your side or a winning lottery ticket? If you are unsure, there is always tarot cards and many other tools to help you uncover exactly who this person is that you are sharing time or space with, but sometimes only time will tell. Although I recommend always following your intuition. The astrology placements discussed in this book will often let you know whether the sparks are likely to be snuffed out – which often happens when there is not enough in your charts to hold the relationship together. Just because someone is a soulmate, doesn't mean the two of you are going to make it long term.

I created a Soulmate Quiz for this very purpose. You will find it at the end of the book and be able to clearly recognize just how much connection you have with your partner by tallying up points. Basically, the more points you have, the more ties that will cement the relationship. But first I want to give you a crash course on reading astrology charts, and a full understanding of soulmate placements. The purpose is to enable you to take the Soulmate Quiz, whether you are at a beginner or advanced level of astrology. So, let's check out that unique blueprint that makes you, YOU!

CHAPTER 2
Pie in the Sky

Astrology can be an amazing study that lasts a lifetime. Ancient Chaldean people followed the stars mapping out when events were likely to happen. They became experts at prediction and passed down their knowledge, however much of it was lost. Astrology continues today with what has been salvaged and is practiced in cultures all over the world. Although there are horoscopes in daily newspapers and magazines, these barely brush the surface, ignoring the depths of astrological study. Many ancients used this science to predict the weather (now called "meteorology"), followed the correct times to heal the body (now called "medicine"), mapped out the sky (now called "astronomy"), studied human behavior (now called "psychology") etc. Some of these practical applications are still used, but the most popular recognition of practicing astrology is its amazing ability to analyze one's character, life purpose, compatibilities with others (called "synastry") and predict the probable future. We will be concentrating mainly on some of these aspects of compatibility, specifically past-life relationships with others (soulmates) that have the potential to become long-term relationships in this life.

To begin, you will need a "Natal Chart" for both you and

your partner. I will talk about how to get these drawn up at the end of this chapter.

WHAT IS A NATAL CHART?

Imagine if you had a blueprint that could map out your entire life. The future choices available to you in each circumstance, your personality, desires, fears and even your physical appearance. Would you want to get your hands on it? Well, a Natal Chart is that very thing. It is a map of you created from the instant you were born. Based on the location, date and time of your birth, your chart shows what was happening in the sky at that very moment. As if you took the sky and flipped it over onto a piece of paper. And the modern way of "drawing" or "casting" your chart is to use a computer program that can instantly do the math for you.

Learning to read a natal chart is as simple or complex as you want to make it. I am hoping that you will find astrology as fascinating as I have. Over the last forty years I have studied my chart and still manage to see new revelations every time I look at it. Although astrology is not limited to just learning about yourself. You can make a chart of the world, a country, another person, your pet, an event or anything else you can dream up.

ZODIAC SOUP

As I mentioned, you can see your entire life in those squiggles on the paper. It is limitless what a chart can show you once you learn to read its core elements. And these elements make up what I call "Zodiac Soup". With soup you have three main ingredients: the filler (veggies/meat/pasta), the seasoning and water. And you need all three to make soup. With just water and filler you have ingredients soaking in water. With just water and seasoning you have broth. And with just seasoning and filler your food is burning on the stove with no water. And so it is, with an astrology chart.

WHAT, WHERE & HOW?

When you learn to read the basic components of your chart, it is like a new world opening up. There is no limit to the amount of information you can find, waiting for your discovery. Like soup, the three main ingredients in every astrology chart are the signs, planets and houses. They represent the "what" (planets), "where" (houses) and "how" (signs) that make up your life. Notice I left out "when". That is predictive astrology and a subject for another book. I will break this down further for you, and I think you will be amazed at how easily these pieces of the puzzle fit together.

What is Happening?

When looking at any area of your life, you will have a "what" that is the subject of any action. The noun playing the starring role in that particular event. And that "what" is the Planets. The planets include: The Sun, Moon (in astrology the Sun and Moon are considered planets), Mercury, Venus, Mars, Jupiter, Saturn, Uranus, Neptune and Pluto. These are seen in your chart in relation to their position to the Sun in the sky. You will have all nine planets in your chart somewhere. They are the active forces that determine *what* is the subject matter – either internally or externally. It is also the "what" that is affected by any event or action. For example, the Moon is related to your emotional needs, so the "what" corresponds to emotional matters. To decipher soulmate placements, you will primarily be working with the planets Sun, Moon, Venus and Mars, (but it is good idea to study all of them and their meanings).

What = The Planets
    Something is happening with:
    (Keywords)
    Sun – Life force, identity, potential, power
    Moon – Needs, emotions, memory, security
    Mercury – Mind, communication, intellect, voice

Venus – Love, money, pleasure, desire
Mars – Action, aggression, passion, drive
Jupiter – Expansion, contraction, luck, travel
Saturn – Restriction, karma, authority, responsibility
Uranus – Unexpected, sudden, unorthodox, electricity
Neptune – Illusion, ecstasy, addiction, dreams
Pluto – Transmutation, explosive, destruction, regeneration

Where is it Happening?

We know "what" is happening – a planet is triggering an event. But *where* is that event taking place? What part of your life? Houses can show you this. The houses are the pie slices you see on a zodiac wheel. It is as if someone cut the sky into pieces and assigned each to represent different areas of life. The lines on each side of a slice are called "cusps". They are dividing lines between each house so you can map when a planet leaves one house and enters the next. Each house is divided into thirty degrees, such as if you were to cut a piece of pie into even narrower slices. These marker increments are the degrees showing exactly where the planet sits in any given house. Did it just cross the cusp and enter? That would mean it would be in the lower degrees. Is it closer to exiting the house? It would be in the higher degrees. More on this later.

SIGNS OF A SOULMATE

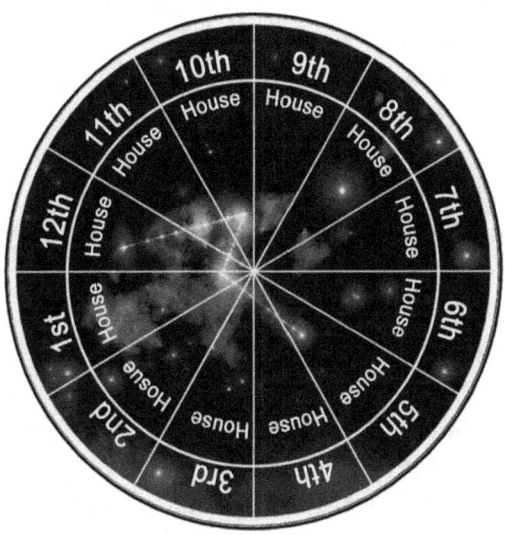

Figure 1 - The Houses

Where = The Houses
Something is happening in the area of:
(Keywords)
1st house – Self, body type, childhood, personality, ego, first impression on others
2nd house – Money, possessions, security, self-worth, greed/generosity, values
3rd house – Communication, siblings, short trips, forms of transportation, school/teaching
4th house – Home, father, old age, real estate, roots, nurturing, country of origin
5th house – Romance, children, creativity, fun, risk taking, drama, sports
6th house - Health, food, work, pets, paternal aunts/uncles, obligations, employees

7th house – Business partners, clients, marriage, grandparents, contracts, BFFs, enemies

8th house – Soulmates, psychic ability, wills, taxes, other people's money, secrets

9th house – Philosophy, religion, legal issues, travel, university, in-laws, international

10th house – Career, reputation, mother, authority figures, homosexuality, public eye

11th house – Network of friends/associates, social circles, main income, hope, other people's children

12th house – Past lives/karma, maternal relatives, unconscious, psychic gifts, large animals, anything that confines you

How is it Happening?

The planets tell "what" is happening. The houses "where" it happens. "How" they tell the story is through the twelve zodiac signs. These are the expressions of the planet, and each sign brings its own set of characteristics. Therefore, a planet will express differently based on what sign it is in. The signs go in order around the outside of the zodiac wheel and represent the ecliptic: Aries, Taurus, Gemini, Cancer, Leo, Virgo, Libra, Scorpio, Sagittarius, Capricorn, Aquarius and Pisces. They relate to constellations as far as mythology or archetypes are concerned, but in Western Tropical astrology they represent where the Sun, planets and stars are in relation to the Sun in its ecliptic path in the sky at any given time. The signs rotate counterclockwise around the chart wheel of houses. When they are in their starting positions, and all lined up nicely (before the clock starts to tick) Aries (being the first sign) will be at zero degrees on the cusp of the first house. It is therefore called the "ruler" of the first house. Taurus being the next sign will line up with the second house and is therefore called the ruler of the second house, and so on.

How = The Signs
A planet will express itself as:
(Keywords)
Aries – Energetic, impatient, courageous, bold
Taurus – Practical, loyal, stubborn, sensual
Gemini – Adaptable, intelligent, cunning, fickle
Cancer – Nurturing, moody, impressionable, instinctive
Leo – Cheerful, creative, regal, dramatic
Virgo – Analytical, critical, detailed, productive
Libra – Indecisive, peacemaker, charming, refined
Scorpio – Passionate, magnetic, transformative, intuitive
Sagittarius – Adventurer, optimistic, reckless, idealistic
Capricorn – Achiever, respectable, reliable, conservative
Aquarius – Eccentric, progressive, unpredictable, humanitarian
Pisces – Psychic, escapist, inspirational, compassionate

WHAT'S YOUR SIGN?

You can learn quite a lot about someone just by knowing their birthdate. When someone casually asks you, "What's your sign," they are asking which sign your Sun is in, which reveals your overall basic character. While it seems an innocent enough question, in all actuality you are giving them a lot of information on how to interact with you. Your Sun Sign reveals your personality, desires, motivations, weaknesses, strengths and fears.

In western astrology, your Sun Sign relates to the constellation the Sun is passing through in its ecliptic "path around the Earth" (from our viewpoint). You will have the characteristics of that sign (See descriptions of the twelve zodiac signs in Chapter 3) as an overarching influence. It is also possible to have other planets in that sign as well. So, when someone asks, "What is your sign," they are referring to the sign your Sun was in when you were born. But there is much more to your story than that! You will be exploring your Sun, Moon, Venus and Mars positions and comparing those to your partner's natal chart.

Find your Sun Sign

The following chart gives the days the Sun spends in each sign. The dates may vary slightly between old school and modern, but this is a general guide to your Sun Sign. If you are born near a cusp, it is always wise to look at your chart for the exact placement of the Sun to make sure you have the correct sign.

Figure 3 - The Sun Signs

Born on a Cusp

If you are born on a day when the Sun is changing signs, you may think you are two signs or confused as to which one you are. You will always be *one* Sun sign or the other, never both. You have all the signs on your wheel, but only one where the Sun is shining. There are some years when the Sun changes signs on a different day than normal, so it is important to run a chart to make sure. It will tell you exactly which sign you are. The Sun reveals what you are aiming to become in this life, based on its sign and house position. It is where you *need* to shine. And it will be important to know it's sign, as that will also reveal possible soulmate connections with a partner.

Confusion over which Sun Sign you are is common for cuspers, because all the signs express somewhere in our chart. Let's take an example of a cusp day: You were born on April 19th on the Aries/Taurus cusp. Your Sun Sign would be assumed to be Aries. But you will need to check to make sure. You may swear that you are more Taurus than Aries, but maybe you have strong Taurus placements in other planets, or a strong Venus, the ruler of Taurus. Another possibility is a lot of planets or energy happening with the 2nd house, the house of Taurus. So, you could have your Sun in Aries, but a lot of Taurus influence elsewhere in the chart. There are times when a person appears to have little to no resemblance to the description of their Sun Sign. This can be for any number of reasons such as the Sun being hidden in the 12th house. This is the house of the unconscious or unexpressed inner self. Therefore, the characteristics are still present but not readily acknowledged or shown in an outer way. Or maybe one of the other planets is expressing stronger than the Sun. These are just some of many possibilities. Your natal chart will clear up any doubt.

CREATING YOUR ZODIAC CHART

Having a natal chart created is very easy. You can get a free printout online at Astro.com. From the menu, choose "Free Horoscopes". Then click on "Horoscope Drawings & Data", then "Chart Drawing Ascendant". (For other programs you would be looking for a "natal chart" and make sure you are using Tropical, and Placidus for the house system.) Next enter your information including name, birth date, time of birth, world location and city/town. When your chart comes up you can click on it to print. Then click "edit birth data" to enter your partner's information.

The research in this book is based off the Placidus House System, which alters your houses a bit to allow for a tilt of the

Earth relative to the ecliptic. If you live closer to the North or South poles you may notice that some of your houses appear larger than others, and that some signs may stretch to cover and influence more than one house, while other signs may be crowded completely inside of a house (intercepted). A good example of this type of skewed look to the houses is the chart of Ann-Margaret, shown in Chapter 11.

What if I Don't Know my Time of Birth?

You can find your time of birth often listed on birth certificates, hospital records, baptismal records a baby book or other types of documentation. If you do not have access to the information, a qualified astrologer can work with you on a Rectification Chart, which will attempt to "rectify" when you were born based on a series of events and dates in your past. You will still be able to take the Soulmate Quiz, but no birth time will eliminate some of the questions.

Interpreting Your Natal Chart

Here is a sample chart of Catherine Jordan, an imaginary person used as an example. Your chart should look relatively similar to hers. Make sure you have a chart created in "Tropical Placidus". If you look under her name and birth information on the left, you will see it listed there.

SIGNS OF A SOULMATE

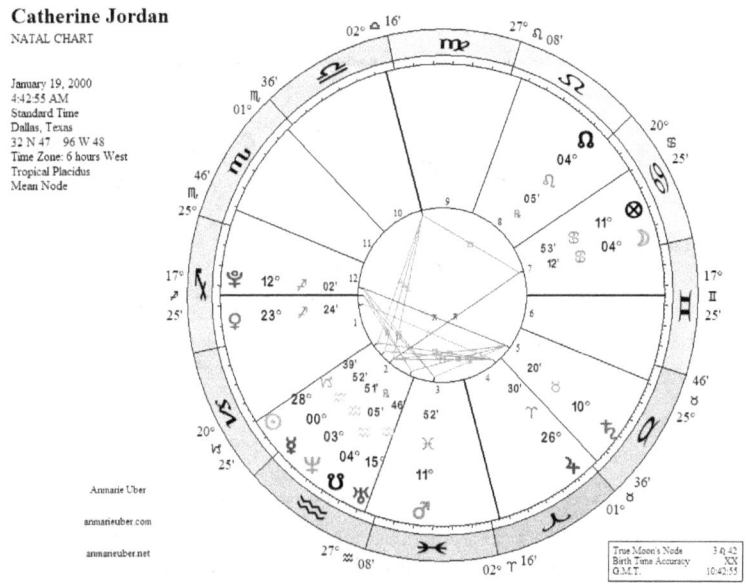

Figure 4 - Sample Chart

In the center of Catherine's wheel, you will see a smaller circle. This represents the Earth and the area around it is the sky at the time of her birth, cut into twelve pieces of pie to represent the houses. These sections correspond to specific areas of her life. The planets are scattered throughout the circle, landing in various houses. The small numbers with the degree signs next to the planets show the measurement of exactly where a planet is in a house. The outer wheel is the ring of signs that continues to turn. Imagine your natal chart as a clock that is continually ticking away. Because of this, the signs will continue to move just like hands on a clock but will not always match up nicely with the houses. They may stop halfway between one house and the next.

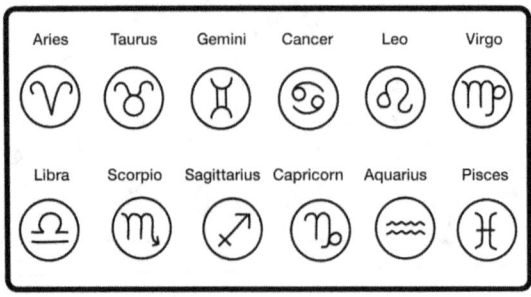

If you look at the outer ring of Catherine's chart, the symbol for Aquarius is at the bottom and spans across most of the 2nd house and partially into the 3rd. Since it crosses the cusp line of the 3rd, it is considered to be "on the cusp of the 3rd house". The 2nd house also has Capricorn so that house would have both Capricorn and Aquarius influences. As the outer ring of signs continues to turn, they change house positions, but will never change their sequential order.

SIGNS OF A SOULMATE

PUTTING THE PUZZLE TOGETHER

The astrology glyphs or symbols represent the planets and signs displayed in the houses. Using the keywords for the planets, houses and signs you can put the pieces of the chart together to make sense.

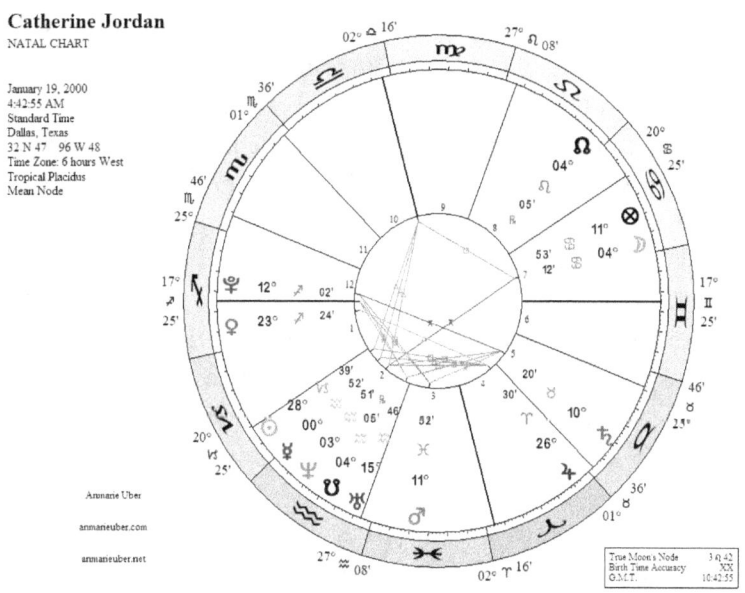

Figure 5 - Sample Chart 2

Catherine's Venus, can tell us about her love preferences in life. Referencing the planet squiggles we see that she has the Venus glyph sitting in the 1st house. Looking at the outer ring of signs, we see Sagittarius overlapping the cusp of her first house. Next to the Venus symbol we also see 23 degrees and a smaller symbol for Sagittarius. So, putting it together - Catherine has Venus in the first house in Sagittarius! Let's read our keywords to see what that means.

The "what" chart below says Venus has to do with love, money, pleasure and desire. The first house of "where" has to do with the physical body, personality and childhood. The "how" is the sign Sagittarius which has to do with adventure, optimism, recklessness and idealism. Let's take one keyword for each. Money (Venus), physical body (1st house) and idealism (Sagittarius). We could say Catherine could be prosperous based on her physical looks and may idealize physical appearances in others. She could possibly be a model or the "face" or representative of a company trying to convey a certain image. Maybe she likes to dress like she has money, or dresses to impress. This would be one way of fitting the keywords together.

When looking at Catherine's 2nd house, I want to point out that the planets aren't always going to be in the same sign as the sign that is on the actual cusp of that house. In the second house, she has Capricorn overlapping the cusp, with Aquarius taking over the second half of the house. She has Sun in Capricorn in the 2nd house, and Mercury, Neptune and Uranus in Aquarius in the 2nd house.

If we wanted to see how Catherine's home life affected her during childhood, we would consider looking specifically at the 4th house which has to do with roots, the father, the home and hearth, and nurturing. She has Jupiter in the 4th house with Aries on the cusp. Jupiter is also in Aries. You would say this as, "Catherine has Jupiter in Aries in the 4th house." Jupiter is a sign of expansion and anything larger than life. Maybe one parent was larger than life to this person. This could be a male because it is the 4th house and the sign Aries is masculine, so possibly her father. Or read in a negative aspect, a controlling domineering male parental influence. More information could be found in the rest of her chart.

What – The Planet Keywords:

Sun – Life force, identity, potential, power

Moon – Needs, emotions, memory, security
Mercury – Mind, communication, intellect, voice
Venus – Love, money, pleasure, desire
Mars – Action, aggression, passion, drive
Jupiter – Expansion, contraction, luck, travel
Saturn – Restriction, karma, authority, responsibility
Uranus – Unexpected, Sudden, unorthodox, electricity
Neptune – Illusion, ecstasy, addiction, dreams
Pluto – Transmutative, explosive, destruction, regeneration

Where – The House Keywords:
1st house – Self, body type, childhood, personality, ego, first impression on others
2nd house – Money, possessions, security, self-worth, greed/generosity, values
3rd house – Communication, siblings, short trips, forms of transportation, school/teaching
4th house – Home, father, old age, real estate, roots, nurturing, country of origin
5th house – Romance, children, creativity, fun, risk taking, drama, sports
6th house - Health, food, work, pets, paternal aunts/uncles, obligations, employees
7th house – Business partners, clients, marriage, grandparents, contracts, BFFs, enemies
8th house – Soulmates, psychic ability, wills, taxes, other people's money, secrets
9th house – Philosophy, religion, legal issues, travel, university, in-laws, international
10th house – Career, reputation, mother, authority figures, homosexuality, public eye
11th house – Network of friends/associates, social circles, main income, hope, other people's children

12th house – Past lives/karma, maternal relatives, unconscious, psychic gifts, large animals, anything that confines you

How – The Sign Keywords:
    Aries – Energetic, impatient, courageous, bold
    Taurus – Practical, loyal, stubborn, sensual
    Gemini – Adaptable, intelligent, cunning, fickle
    Cancer – Nurturing, moody, impressionable, instinctive
    Leo – Cheerful, creative, regal, dramatic
    Virgo – Analytical, critical, detailed, productive
    Libra – Indecisive, peacemaker, charming, refined
    Scorpio – Passionate, magnetic, transformative, intuitive
    Sagittarius – Adventure, optimism, reckless, idealistic
    Capricorn – Achiever, respectable, reliable, conservative
    Aquarius – Eccentric, progressive, unpredictable, humanitarian
    Pisces – Psychic, escapist, inspirational, compassionate

MORE SQUIGGLES

When you get a chart printed, it may come with a graph that contains the symbols for the planets listed somewhere outside of the wheel. On this graph are glyphs to represent aspects between the planets – basically showing how they get along. Will they be naturally attuned? At odds with each other? These planetary relationships are called *aspects*. The particular planets involved will determine what type of issues you are dealing with and how to work on tough areas of your life, as well appreciating what comes easy for you.

SIGNS OF A SOULMATE

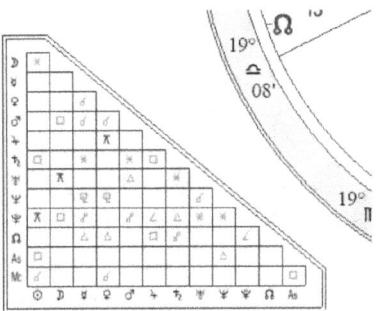

Figure 6 - The Aspects in graph form

The aspects are shown at the center of your chart. Sometimes it can look like a plate of spaghetti.

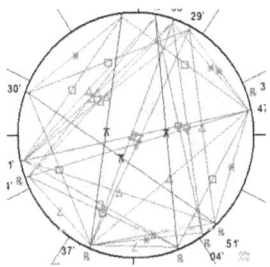

Figure 7 - The Aspects in the center of a chart

Some of the following aspects are considered when comparing soulmate placements - the trine, opposition, conjunct and parallel which will be discussed in a later chapter.

ASPECTS

Here are a few of the main astrology aspects:

Trine (Easy Accord) – When two planets are 120 degrees apart it is called a trine. This aspect creates a natural harmony and understanding, and you can be lucky in the areas represented. On the downside, this aspect can lead to boredom from a lack of challenges, making things too easy or taking them for granted.

Sextile (Opportunities) – If two planets are 60 degrees apart, it fosters an amicable relationship between them. They don't share as much empathy as the trine, but situations in those areas run smoothly. (Roughly within 6 degrees will count as a sextile.)

Quincunx (Annoyances) – Planets 150 degrees apart create the quincunx aspect that creates compulsory behavior, obsessiveness and delusional tendencies. These are things that drive you crazy and how you drive others batty. The planets create situations that need to be constantly adjusted to, and you will have to learn to change and go with the flow or you will make yourself miserable. (Roughly 3 degrees difference is still considered a Quincunx.)

SIGNS OF A SOULMATE

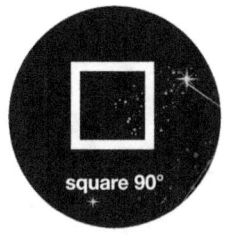

Square (Challenges) - This aspect creates a 90 degree angle of clashes. This is a dead end, stalemate or stop sign that must be worked through and overcome. On the positive side, the more you work through these planetary conflicts, the stronger and more evolved you become. These planets will continue to butt heads but over time these become your strengths.

Opposition (Complementary) – This is a 180 degree aspect which happens when two planets are on opposite sides of the zodiac wheel. Oppositions are opposing forces that must reconcile their differences to become best friends that eventually complement each other. The key to this aspect is learning to develop the traits represented by both planets, especially those that are repressed – the ones you think you lack or deny.

Conjunct (Power Play) – If two planets are 0 degrees apart, it means they are right on top of each other. This creates a battle for dominance, and so the qualities of each planet become greatly enhanced as they strive to outshine each other. It is a power struggle, and if the two planets represented do not normally get along it can become a very challenging aspect to live with. (Roughly 10 degrees difference is still considered a conjunction.)

CHAPTER 3

The 12 Signs of Valentines

To have a committed lasting relationship with another person, it helps to understand your own strengths and weaknesses as well as your partner's. A general harmony in your basic natures is best. You could be opposites or think the same way about things but there needs to be some consistent flow between the two of your personalities to make it for the long haul. In an astrology chart the planets, signs and houses help make these connections. The four planets Sun, Moon, Venus and Mars create a foundation of friendship and sexual attraction that can help two people stay together. Planets will get along, clash or ignore each other.

In this chapter I will be discussing the basic nature of these four planets expressing through each of the twelve signs Aries through Pisces. The Sun Sign reflects not only the type of person you both are but how you respond and function in a general way to the world around you. The Sun expresses the characteristics of the signs in their truest form and shines on the whole chart. The Moon represents an individual's emotional state and what they need from a relationship. Venus reflects how an individual loves and wants to be loved. Mars shows how an individual expresses passion. It is interesting to note that sometimes a man will seem to express his Mars sign more than his Sun or a woman her Venus.

THE ROLES WE PLAY

Each sign has a masculine or feminine quality, and the characteristics of that sign will play out differently through a man or woman. In all relationships, one person is playing the "male" and the other the "female". What do I mean by this? For example, if you are in a gay relationship, consider which partner is displaying the more masculine active, protective giving energy and who is playing the passive receptive feminine. A person will choose to personify a masculine or feminine energy (we are not talking about physical male/female bodies) based on many factors that have formed their behavior and preferences. These can include the sex they were in a past life (which may or may not be the same as now) which predetermines the sex they relate with or convey as well as their sexual preferences. Also, societal influences and conditioning, emulating a role model or the values or pressures of upbringing can be instrumental in having a greater propensity toward a male or female expression. A male or female essence is in everything. There is a masculine and feminine quality to the nature and shape of most plants. If you study Chinese face reading, there are characteristics of the face that display this masculine or feminine energy. Such as, a long nose is considered a feminine feature because length is female expansion, whereas a small nose is contracting energy and considered masculine. The planets and signs are the same. They take on male or female characteristics.

For example, if your Sun is in a masculine sign and you are a female, you may take on a more masculine role in relationships. Or you may compensate for weak male energy in a partner. You could find it difficult to be maternal if you enjoy the masculine side of yourself more than the feminine. I see this in a lot of straight women who dominate the traditional relationship and do all the giving. Which usually draws them into relationships with men who are "takers" and are playing a more passive feminine role. Society may expect men to be the bread winner or giver/supporter/protector of the family, but a man who resents that could attract women who take on the more dominant or masculine role for him. This can play out in any number of ways. Another possibility could be that someone has incarnated into many past lives as say, a male. They are born into this life as a female. They don't feel connected to a female energy expression and long to be the male active role. There is no one reason why someone chooses to express the way they do, but the signs do have male and female expressions.

For simplicity, the following descriptions will use established male and female perspectives as in a man and woman. You will have to interpret them to fit your specific relationship. For a more detailed explanation of the use of "male" and "female", please see the "note" that follows.

Note: I am using terminology in this chapter for the sake of ease of writing. And to describe certain qualities. My descriptions of these zodiac signs apply to all relationships, whether gay, straight or any other description. The terms "male", "man", "woman" and "female" all relate to the essence of masculine or feminine which has nothing to do with an individual's physical body type. Every person will display a dominant masculine or feminine energy. Everyone has both male and female traits, but one will be dominant. This decides the "role" you are playing in the relationship.

What is masculine and feminine? Masculine is movement. The giving driving energy. Feminine is the receiving or passive energy. Masculine takes the lead. Masculine protects. Feminine absorbs, nurtures and adjusts. I am a straight female and have almost always had to play both the masculine and feminine role in relationships, because the straight males I was with should have been playing their masculine role but were expecting me to support them financially and otherwise. So, in essence they were really playing the child. I was not happy in these relationships having to be the male energy when I desire to express feminine. But I was raised to "do for myself", "don't accept help", "do it all" and so I attracted men who wanted to be a child and sit around while I did everything for them. I had to learn to embrace my feminine energy and be okay with receiving, and demanding reciprocal give-and-take. In a gay relationship two of the same sex are attracted to each other but one will almost always be expressing either the masculine or feminine to a greater degree and will take on that role in the relationship. Sometimes partners exchange their roles over time based on life circumstances, but that is not the norm.

What essence do you identify with – what do you normally feel comfortable in – the masculine or feminine role? Decide which you are, so you are not forced into a relationship that is not natural to you, what you prefer or what you were told you needed to be.

The following descriptions consider people who exist in a *relatively healthy psychological range.* They are not meant to be ascribed to sociopaths, psychopaths or destructive mindsets of those who desire to hurt others or perpetrate their character flaws. I am focusing here on healthy partners with good intentions and character – emotionally and mentally healthy with normal issues and problems. Not major character flaws that lead to extreme issues, trauma or deliberate drama that would drag your life down, as well as those around you. These type of "red flag" people tend to pull you into messes that you get trapped in or spend an extremely long time trying to fix or escape from. To clarify again, the following section is describing individuals on the healthier end of the spectrum.

SIGNS OF A SOULMATE

ROMANCING THE SIGNS

ARIES

*"Aries has a heart of gold
In battle they will never fold
Stir their passion and name your plight
And once in motion, for you they fight."*

Aries the Ram is a masculine cardinal fire sign displaying the culmination of energy, passion and drive. Since these folks are low on patience, I will make this quick. Never tell an Aries they can't do something, or to "slow down". These individuals have the gift of endless energy. This sign is the epitome of the testosterone driven battle-scarred planet Mars that rules it. The four "Cs" are what make these people tick and get out of bed in the morning - conflict, conquest, challenge and conquer. They are the heroes of the zodiac. The soldier that is ready to fight the enemy. So, pull out your word swords and fight them a little bit. They love it. Aries is also the romantic knight in shining armor that rides in on his horse (males and females alike) to save the day. Aries seems capable of going on little to no sleep, keeping one eye open for any ensuing battle that might present itself. Without a cause or purpose Aries can become a deflated balloon leading to possible lethargy and depression, which is so out of character for them. A sad state for this otherwise virile and valiant champion. I would be the last person to tell them to slow down, but it would be tremendously helpful if they could become more aware of their surroundings and the people in their peripheral. Before rushing off to the next appointment...they are usually cutting it close on time...pause and acknowledge other people and their feelings first. Slow down and communicate. Don't expect everyone to want what you want. Not everyone shares the ram's opinions and passions or can match their endless bursts of energy. Not that Aries deliberately intends to ignore anyone, they are just in such a hurry that...never mind...they have already left the building.

Aries Male

When you take an already male astrology sign that is ruled by a warrior planet and express it through male energy you get the champion. The person who is willing to jump into the mire and rescue the damsel in distress. The hero. The soldier who will win the battle by willpower alone. Too much Aries and you get the chauvinist. The single-mindedness of self, which can come across as selfishness (but this tends to play out a bit more with the female, if the Aries Sun is badly aspected). These men are extremely confident unless they have been influenced to believe otherwise. And have a lot of stamina and passion in the bedroom. They like things hard and fast. Fast cars, rough sex, you get the idea – so slap them around a bit. They like it and anything else that gives them an adrenaline rush and a challenge. Allow Aries a space to control at home, such as an office or somewhere that is solely theirs.

To romance an Aries male, be bold. Walk right up and tell them who is boss. Then enjoy the show as they take the bait and fight to prove who is in charge. They like to work for things. Don't be afraid to dress sexy but be respectable too, with an air of innocence about you. Just enough of a mix to entice their desire to unravel or unwrap your mysteries. They want a challenge in a nicely wrapped package. And lots of passion. They want to ask the question, "Who is this person and why do I desire him/her?" Aries is looking to see if you are the "one" they have been waiting for, who can occupy that empty place on the 'ole partner pedestal. Whether you embody all their idealized dreams. Light their flame and they will ride into battle and face the hounds of hell to fight for you.

Aries Female

The Aries female is always willing to help a family or friend and can be amazingly selfless and generous, if you can tie them down long enough to let them know you are having troubles. But the female Aries can be typical of service to self because the feminine aspect is receptive. So, the pursuing of their own goals, wants and needs come first. On the other hand, these women are masters at analyzing their shortcomings and learning to overcome weak areas in their characters (thus making them some of the most evolved and enlightened beings you know, as far as self-awareness). This is the Mars energy desiring to understand weakness (even in themselves), so that strength for the battle of life is increased and success guaranteed. The unevolved Aries female replenishes their energy supplies by siphoning it off others. They drain other people by triggering dramatic emotional reactions which refill their own fuel supply. This is one of the few "used" things Aries will take – your energy. They like new things or something that is not covered in someone else's vibes.

When romancing an Aries female - first you had better be able to keep up. They like verbal sparring (arguing) or a good old-fashioned fight. It is part of the passion and stimulation for when things get a bit boring or not going the Aries way. Female rams like a man that can stand up to them while maintaining an elusive quality and also being highly romantic. If you can figure all that out, you have them. Keep this female guessing by being unavailable one day and showing up the next with red roses (or a gift connected to her Venus sign) all googly-eyed and hopelessly at their beck and call. It's a roller coaster – play hard to get but available at the same time. But ultimately be willing to back down and allow the Aries to take charge and lead the relationship.

Long term love possibilities for Sun in Aries:

Aries, Leo, Sagittarius, Scorpio, Pisces. Virgo too if both parties are on the same spiritual path. Libra is a good partner if you overcome the challenges of opposite personalities. Cancer is a good match if you are both willing to grow from and face (accept) your differences. (These sign placements can also be found in a house, or another compatible planet as shown later in this book.)

Mean Astrology: I lead because I have more energy than twenty of you put together, so I am already in the lead. Besides, I don't have time to wait on the turtles. I've got a race to win.
 If you don't do it my way you will regret it.

- Day: Tuesday
- Number: 9
- Metal: Iron
- Colors: Red, scarlet, crimson

Aries Soul Imprint: "I am the hero."

Body Rulerships: Head, eyes, brain, pituitary, skull, upper jaw, carotid arteries, muscular strength.

Aries Careers (also look to your Venus sign): Military, medical doctor, optometrist, engineer, athlete, any type of body therapist, entrepreneur, artsy professions, carpenter, researcher, law enforcement, hairstylist, brain surgeon, fire fighter, journalist, entertainer.

> *"Is there a prince out there*
> *With golden hair*
> *Waiting to whisk me away*
> *On his chariot of angel's wings?*
> *Is my true love there*
> *with the raven hair*
> *To sing me to sleep*
> *And kiss my eyes*
> *And tell me he is happy*
> *To be alive?*
> *Is my red-haired knight*
> *Waiting to fight*
> *The angels of darkness*
> *To find me here*
> *dreaming of him*
> *In my tower of loneliness?*
> *Is there none, then*
> *That can sweep me off my feet*
> *Make me meet*
> *My maker in his eyes*
> *For such a true one*
> *I have desired*
> *A pure one*
> *One as strong as the*

> *midday sun*
> *who can light up my life*
> *Casting away*
> *shadows of doubt*
> *Clouding around every hopeful*
> *beau crossing my path.*
> *Can you not blast*
> *Your way into my life"*[1]

Moon in Aries

Welcome to the instant gratification crowd. These folks do not like to wait...for anything. They needed it to happen yesterday and while we are at it, let's get tomorrow done with too. From an emotional standpoint, this may mean Moon in Aries does not have much staying power, or the emotions could run hot and cold. But make no mistake, they are very demanding while they *are* feeling something. There is a sense of rushing in decisions as well. If they get emotional about money, it could lead to frivolousness and acting without thinking. These people can come across with a childlike innocence or openness that can be refreshing. Aries Moons have a need to rescue something. Relationships are all about heroes and villains. They need to get reactions from you – and they could use a good argument right about now to heat things up a bit. If you want to get them to do something, turn everything into a competition. Let them know *someone else* is winning. "You don't want to lose, do you?" And give a little finger push to their shoulder, "Bet you can't beat me." They need a good dare now and then. But fight them when they try to be too controlling.

Venus in Aries

They love people who are up to the challenge. They also value honesty and people who can get right to the point. Let them know where you stand. No vagueness please. Tell them you love them but don't be a pushover about it. Give them a bit of a chase. They can't wait to take control. Don't let them. Argue with them. Venus in Aries wants to put their partner on a pedestal, but only after they have won you. Then they want the challenge of keeping you, so don't make it too easy. Venus in Aries loves the "new and shiny" and that includes you, so keep the relationship honest but keep them guessing. They love sporting events, or any activity that is challenging or requires creativity – just keep things moving.

When you take the words impulsive, impatient, controlling optimistic and easily duped, and combine them with money, you may or may not have a problem. But it summarizes Venus in Aries with a pocket of cash. In finance, like everything else, Aries wants to take the "quick way round".

In bed they can be aggressive and no nonsense. Let's not waste time, shall we? Unless you want them to chase you around the bedroom first or play a game of "hard to get". Then they are all in as far as taking their time.

Ideal date: Playing video games or a sport together, rock climbing or anything edgy, competitive or adventurous.

Mars in Aries

Here is a double whammy of energy, as Mars the planet of drive is in its home sign of Aries the sign of forward movement. This placement's motto is "Do it now" or "Right now," as my Aries Mother would say. This Mars can outperform you if what is required is endurance and determination. They have an endless supply of both. They are the type to take action and get things done – as fast as humanly possible. They come at you head-on, like a ram ready to butt you out of the way or to get their way. They are not always subtle and may not mince words. Sports or any activity is done with a competitive spirit. They have the chivalry gene and won't hesitate to throw down their coat over the proverbial puddle. This Mars is burning with get-up-and-go, at times not knowing what to do with their surplus of energy. Mars in Aries always seems to be raging about something, but the anger is usually short-lived. They believe in "let's fight fair and get it done with".

TAURUS

"Taurus' slow and grounded love
Fits around you like a glove
To win their heart go the slow way 'round
And silently they're yours without making a sound."

Taurus the Bull is a fixed earth sign, which means they are slow to action, and approach things very methodically. Practicality is their middle name. Until the bull gets stirred up. Then it is best that you put down that red cape and step your matador ass out of the way. Everything was fine until you mistook the sweet-tempered bull for stupid. They are anything but. And they are not pushovers. Their logic could blow away weak irrational yapping any day. The bull has listened long enough so sit down and shut up. Something interesting I have noticed about Taurus (including Leo) is that they have some type of inborn protection around them. Like they could walk through the fires of hell and a demon would run the other way. They usually have a great physical constitution and can outwork most people. However, the bull has trouble understanding why other people can't keep up or carry the same load. Taurus is dependable and their word is usually reliable. You can take it to the bank - one of Taurus' favorite places. They will be there for you, no matter what – unless you mistreat them of course. A bull is here to experience and decide what has value to them. Early in life that may be the material world, finances and their attachment to the security it provides. But at some point, Taurus will desire real love, and pursue being loved as their most important goal. Even overriding or losing material possessions if it came to that. But hopefully it never does. Taurus wants to hold on to both.

Male Taurus

The male Taurus is expressing through a feminine sign. These males like to be admired by the opposite sex (or same sex for gay couples). They want to feel attractive, loved for who they are, and borderline worshipped by the partner. If the attention wanes, their usually loyal eye can stray to another woman who will fill that need. They look for someone else to move on to first, before leaving a relationship, as the need to feel loved is paramount. In work/career they choose the safe route, or something that will guarantee they will have the amount of money they need to buy their security. Depending on how much the male bull loves you will determine whether he is willing to step up and take a hit for you. He can just as easily disappear when he is too quick to judge. This is where the famous stubbornness comes in – he has expectations down to the detail of how his partner should be and if you step outside of that, his eye starts to roam. And once his bull-headed mind is made up, whether selfish or not, it is highly difficult if not impossible to get him to reconsider or apologize. A great way to get this man's consideration early on, is through food and bodily comforts. Fulfill the five senses. Make him feel at ease and comfortable. Then, while he is in a meat and potatoes haze, ask for what you want.

Female Taurus

This female is true blue. Loyalty runs in her veins and is expected in return. She demands to be accepted for who she is, faults and all. And someone overly critical of her is a fool, as she represents one of the most loyal friends and reciprocal lovers. In a crisis you can bet she is first on the scene. She is the glue that holds the family together. However, disrespect her, take her for granted or fail to praise her and you might find that the rug of solidarity and safety has been pulled out from under you - the Taurus female who had your back is gone. She has common sense – loads of it – and can be stubborn at times, but it is usually for a good reason that was well thought over. Or maybe it is something that she just doesn't want to do. She is usually great with the finances, organization and keeping the stability. She craves security, safety and the "known" and is not one to take risks. This female is looking for the tried-and-true in a partner, and ultimately love.

Long term love possibilities for Sun in Taurus: Taurus, Virgo, Capricorn, Gemini, Libra. Sagittarius too if both parties are on the same spiritual path. Scorpio is a good partner if you overcome the challenges of opposite personalities. Aquarius is a good match if you both are willing to grow together from and face (accept) your differences. (These sign placements can also be found in a house, or another compatible planet as shown later in this book.)

Mean Astrology – I do what I want, because I have reasoned it out and found the safest route. And because I can. You won't be able to budge me.

I lead because I rationally and practically analyze each person and situation to see if they match my high code of ethics. If not, I do what I believe to be right and what will bring me and my loved one's safety. I lead because people rely on my common sense.

- Day: Friday
- Number: 6
- Metal: Copper
- Colors: Blue

Taurus Soul Imprint: "I possess security."

Body Rulerships: Throat, face, nose, mouth, tongue, facial bones, ears, neck, cerebellum, lower jaw, thyroid, tonsils, larynx, clavicle, vocal cords.

Taurus Careers (also look to your Venus sign): (Taurus will usually migrate toward a secure job – not necessarily what they want to do) Investor, banker, photographer, landscaper, graphic artist, art director, jeweler, beauty sales or artistry, farmer, singer/musician, treasurer, corporate environment, manager, headhunter.

>"Take this heart, and make of it, a new one.
>   With your smile, teach it to sing again,
>   the song of Love.
>   With your kiss restore the rhythm of its beat.
>   Mold me, as a potter would a lump of clay,
>   into a cup, from which only your lips may drink.
>
>Take this heart, and make of it a new one.
>   With your hands, knit together the frayed edges,
>   worn away by years of neglect and exposure.
>   With your caress upon my brow, and your head upon my breast,
>   breathe into me the breath of Life, that I may live again.
>
>Take this heart, and make of it a new one.
>   And when you have, as you have,

please place it beside your own,
that this heart may know once more,
it does not beat in vain."[2]
(Written by a Taurus to his soulmate)

Moon in Taurus

The "certifiably proven", "third-party tested" and "highly recommended" is what makes these people comfortable, and they want to feel like they know you first before getting involved or sharing tender feelings. They are interested in a sure thing. For anything outside that category, Moon in Taurus takes their time, checking out all the angles to make sure the coast is clear, and the family is safe. These bull moons hang on forever, so they need to trust you first before they let you enter their fold. Their home environment is like a stronghold in the storm. It needs to be a place of creature comforts and refuge. Protection is the name of the game. And fielding off life's arrows requires planning ahead of time. They need someone who can strategize with them or at least be part of a solid plan forward. You can depend on Taurus Moon's love to endure. Their feelings stick to you like a bur on your pants leg that doesn't want to let go until you literally tear it off. They are loyal when they care, and indifferent when they don't.

Venus in Taurus

This is Venus in its home sign of Taurus. These people value things that age well. Like fine food and a fine wine, quality takes time. And a quality relationship also takes time to build, so they go the slow way round. One step following another. Venus in Taurus wants to make sure that you are a reliable bet to place their hopes on. They want to make sure the relationship is going to last, while still having time to back out if it looks like a potential partner may turn out to be a loser. These folks also feel comfortable with the permanent, foreseeable and enduring. They like things predictable and prefer to know outcomes ahead of time. Or at least be able to forecast a good guess. These Venus folks also have an artistic eye, appreciating items of good form and quality.

Venus in Taurus may choose to earn their money in low-risk investments or traditional vocations. They like to spend money on good quality items, large purchases that have lasting value and art.

In lovemaking, Venus in Taurus has an earthy sensual expression and enjoys physical touching or caressing. They have stamina and endurance in bed. If they enter a relationship, they intend to be loyal, but can also be a bit possessive.

Ideal date: Eating their favorite food, relaxing at home, snuggling in front of the tube, massages, art shows, shopping and going out for cocktails.

Mars in Taurus

The planet of energy and drive slows down in Taurus the sign that goes about things in a slow and methodical way. This sign placement is going to get the job done but on their own timing and in their own way. Their style is steadfast, dutiful and unwavering. They have goals like everybody else and have every intention of achieving them, but what's the rush? Taurus Mars people are the epitome of patience and if you push them when they are not ready to act it will be like moving a wall of granite. They believe the best in life is worth waiting for. Their actions prove their loyalty, and if they are romancing you, expect plenty of hugs, cuddles and kisses. When they really love you, they have planned for and included you in their future.

GEMINI

*"Gemini flits and Gemini flirts
Looking for light-hearted convo and quirks
But unawares their heart you will catch
If you are special enough to open the latch."*

Gemini the twins is an airy cardinal air sign with masculine qualities. They like to do things *with* someone else and bring out the good or evil twin based on circumstances. If you are worthy, they may entrust you with the sweet innocent twin – the side of themselves they bury and protect. The evil twin can come out for bad people. It is how they survive. Geminis can literally shrug off situations that would lay anyone else low. They have their head in the clouds and their noses into everyone's business. Not *because* they are nosy, but rather they have a need to know what is going on. They want all the details, and they gather more and more until a picture/pattern of their environment comes together, and every question gets answered. In fact, these people can predict the future based on millions of pieces of information floating around in their mind that all come together somehow. Interconnecting into a magical formula that spits out a likely outcome. They do this effortlessly, as it is part of their very nature. And knowing what is coming, or how a person is likely to react is what guides them to their next action. It is what helps their world to make sense. When it comes to love, this attention to noticing all the details kicks into overdrive and they have an immediate sense of whether you are soulmate material based on thousands of data bits that are computing the likeliness of lasting love. So, fill dear Gemini in on the latest gossip and don't deprive their thriving minds. Throw them a scrap or two. They want who went where and how, wearing what and why they left when they did. And say it poetically, phonetically and energetically giving a rhyme for their time and they will be yours forever. Be kind and feed that eternal hunger for info. Understand they are storing the many details to continually formulate the world around them. And if you do leave any information out, they will be sure to hammer you for more. Occasionally you get the silent types that sit and stare, waiting for you to fill the empty chasm of conversation…and you do. Because the silence is deafening. But what better way to get someone talking? Gemini knows. And their seemingly shy smug smile grows larger as it dawns on you that you just revealed every deep dark hidden secret relegated to the private and off-limits areas of your mind as well as blabbing out where Aunt Dorothy really goes, when she says she is heading to knitting class.

Gemini Male

If you feel like this man is just playing with your emotions, don't take it personally. It is just a bored male twin, still looking for his soulmate, and he is either in the process of determining if you are it or has already determined you are not it. Let him run his process and be thankful that he did you a favor of letting you know you are not "the one". But beware. Gemini males have a way of coming back into your life in the meantime until they do find their soulmate. Close the door and do not let him in. He is not there because he changed his mind about you. Gemini has an inner radar that will let him know when he meets her, and if you ain't it, you ain't it. If you take on the role as "fill-in" and he does meet the soulmate, you go bye-bye. Gemini man is looking for the perfect woman. Usually someone beautiful by worldly standards if possible. If you aren't considered model beautiful but he still wants you, no worries. You don't have to live up to that ideal. Just be you. It depends on that predetermined vision he harbors in his mind. Really what he is looking for is the perfect fit for *himself*. You have heard that the Gemini male has two sides. The twins. This split off is for the preservation of the inner self. One part is the pure innocent child self that remains uncorrupted by the world. The other is the warrior self that can fight back to protect the child self or be bad to scare others off the trail. The air sign male does this because Gemini has analyzed the world and realized very quickly that if he lets the innocent loving part of himself out in the open too often it will get crushed. So, the bad Gemini comes out to play quite often, deflecting any potential bullies. Depending on the situation or who they are dealing with, the Gemini man presents either the bad twin or the good twin. Ultimately, what they are hoping for is to find the perfect partner who they can open up with and let the innocent self out where it is in safe hands. A true meeting of the minds, hearts and souls.

Gemini Female

These women are as loyal as the Female Taurus, but if you do them wrong one too many times, the door will slam in your face and there is no turning back. Unlike the Gemini males, this female will play a relationship out to the bitter end. If they have given you their heart – which was possibly a lengthy or well-thought-out process – they are not going to give up so easily. They hold back in giving love, because they know once they accept you, they are all-in. And they will give their all. If you trample on them, they will try to understand. Try to relate. They try anything and everything. But if they realize you just want to hurt them, they will at some point grudgingly accept that reality. This intelligent Mercury female is not going to sit and take your abuse forever. Once they are done, they are done. The females are similar to the males in that they examine and test others for value and worth. But the females go about it in a much different way. They can be cold or hold themselves back while they analyze you from a distance. This doesn't mean it will be a slow process for them to decide whether you are worthy of their time, love and tender hearts. But once they do, Gemini females are extremely loyal to their friends, family and partners, and will do everything in their power to help you if they can. These women are very much in their heads, managing unbelievable amounts of details that only they can organize and make sense of. Sometimes this can lead to mental strain or breakdowns, depending. Gemini females are social and need contact with the outside world. She needs access to information no matter how uncomfortable, because all those details add up to patterns so that she can read the world around her. She has an uncanny ability like the Taurus woman to call a spade a spade – remember that other twin is there and not afraid to call out a bully. But usually, she is just a tender heart wanting to connect. So, don't be that guy who messes it up.

Long Term love possibilities for Sun in Gemini:

Gemini, Libra, Aquarius, Taurus, Capricorn. Scorpio too if both parties are on the same spiritual path. Sagittarius is a good partner if you overcome the challenges of opposite personalities. Virgo is a good match if you are both willing to grow together from and face (accept) your differences. (These sign placements can also be found in a house, or another compatible planet as shown later in this book.)

. . .

Mean Astrology - I lead usually because the leader is not doing a good job. I only follow when absolutely necessary because either I have to, or the person I am following is highly intelligent.

I am actually just doing what I want and making you think I am following the rules.

- Day: Wednesday
- Number: 5
- Metal: Mercury
- Colors: Glittery, silver and platinum

Gemini Soul Imprint: "I think to know."

Body Rulerships: Lungs, nervous system, shoulders, arms, hands.

Gemini Careers (also look to your Venus sign): Tourism, media, negotiation, politics, sales, writers, radio, television, publishing, transportation, pilot, travel industry, hospitality, mechanic, technology, public relations, scientist, teacher.

"We are one
And we are three
The magic trinity
The perfect numerology
Leaving duality behind
Its closed doors of chaos
Opening wide
To the third dimensional side
Of things
Of us
Of joining
And spreading wings
Toward our journey
To the self
That is three.

> You and me.
> Salt, Sulphur and Mercury."[3]

Moon in Gemini

They have a driving need to know eeevvveerryytthhiinngg. And desire to be around people, intermingling. Getting access to what is out there – what is happening. Turn on the television, hand them a gossip mag and pull up a news video and they are happy to bounce from one topic to another, absorbing it all on high speed. This moon can rattle back to you all the specifics putting complex pieces of information together quickly and easily. Tell me what you know, so I can *know*, and move on to the next person who has more news. *And* let's not even talk about multitasking abilities. Want to win their heart? Let this lunar twin talk and keep the conversation informative from your end – stay up to date. Be a mover and a shaker. And for god's sake say something interesting. Their insatiable craving for information includes you – they want to know where you are, when you are, how you are, what you are and anything else you can tell them about your whereabouts. Don't leave a single thing out. They love foreign languages and often have the Mercury talent of a silver tongue, able to pick up accents, or are great mimickers. Whisper in their ear in Swahili, Mandarin or say something exotic, and they are yours forever.

Venus in Gemini

Although they can be a bit of a flirt and a tease this Venus sign's true love is witty conversations, small talk - any kind of talk – they don't care. They want information and exchange. Curiosity killed the cat, and Venus in Geminis have not learned to curb the temptation to pry too far lest they discover something heavy or serious. Any kind of intelligence turns them on, so get your smart pants on and learn a big word or two. Even the abnormally quiet Venus Geminis are beaming with a knowing sparkle in their eyes when anyone flashes some clever wit their way. They have changing tastes, as variety is the spice of life.

With finances a Gemini Venus can let cash flow through their fingers as quickly as the speed of their thoughts. They can be frivolous or irresponsible with cash leading right to the poorhouse. And then yawn at the worriers with an air of nonchalance as they just as effortlessly bounce back from pauperdom. Luck has a way of finding Venus in Gemini, as it does their opposite sign Sagittarius.

As far as romance, talking in bed turns them on, and they love to kiss. Anything you can do with your mouth is a win. Turn out the lights as they can escape at the slightest distraction. But don't smother them once you are done. They prefer to be out of bed as soon as the petting stops. Try more talking while you keep them snuggling for another two minutes.

Ideal Date: The sign of the twins may enjoy a double date, anywhere there is sparkling conversation, a road trip, watching the latest movie, or hanging out at the local coffee shop.

Mars in Gemini

The planet of action expressing through the sign of the intellectual communicator means their actions, passions and motivations are tied to the movement of information. You might find them reading a book. Boredom is death to these people and they seek stimulation and a changing scenery preferably with a variety of interesting things to see and learn along the way. Even if they are not physically active, you can be sure their minds are processing details a mile a minute, devouring masses of information while spinning mental cartwheels of joy. Their facial expressions may reveal little of this whirlwind and they serenely smile as if nothing is happening. Until Gemini Mars is ready to pass that information on. Then they are eager to find an audience of listening ears. These Mars people probably have tons of friends as they continually make the rounds to their ever-growing circle. And nothing gets them moving like a question they don't have an answer to, or an offer of adventure that dropped into their lap. Busy, busy, busy. Mars in Gemini loves to parry or compete with words, whether written or spoken, and may turn out a lovely poem or flowery endearments in romance. Although following through on those words and promises may be another story.

✦

CANCER

"Cancer is a mood that must be learned
Its changes, intensities and frequent turns
Until you sidle up to their emotional surprise
Gradually winning their love and gaining the prize."

Cancer the crab is a feminine water sign of cardinal action, their hearts centered around the home, hearth and family. They are ruled by the moon and usually have a highly developed intuition. All Cancers need some kind of home base. These are sensitive creatures that want to get to know you slowly, before fully opening up emotionally and revealing their true feelings. Cancer is a nurturing mothering sign that rules parenting, homeland and children. Often Cancers can be found working in real estate or something connected to the home such as interior design, house repair or working from a home base. Domestic bliss is sacred. Many prefer to live around water. Cancer's emotions run with the quickly moving moon that changes signs, every two and a half days. This is why they get called moody (or moony) and if their ruling Moon is also in a sign of water, the mood swings can be very unpredictable and intense to deal with. Cancers want to turn relationships inside out and examine them from all angles. They alternate between mothering a loved one or playing the child who needs to be nurtured. Most of their interactions center around this child/parent theme, including Cancer bosses often seeing their employees as their "children" who need looking after. But remember, whether they are your boss, parent, child, lover or friend – Cancer is super psychic and will always know what you are up to. That is if they care or take the time to pay attention. Running off to the next school bake sale, taking the kids to soccer practice, surprising a friend with a birthday cake and a million other things tend to get in the way. They are notorious for taking on too much.

Cancer Male

Because Cancer is a feminine sign with intense lunar emotions, many men with this placement find it hard to function in the world. They may cover or bury their more tender sides, to appear tough to the bullies (everyone else). They definitely need an outlet for their emotional selves. Otherwise, they can conceal emotion to the point where it causes problems later or creates unhealthy forms of escape. And to say these crabby males have moods…they get their moon phases just like women and are often misunderstood because of it. But if you try to give them confidence or validation for their emotions, they run. Cancer men often look to a woman to take over (mother) or be in charge. The mother is revered in a Cancer male's life. She is from whom he formulates all his opinions on women, and how he will treat a future partner. It is not uncommon for a male Cancer to get married and there be a competition of sorts between the time he spends with his mother and time with his spouse. Cancer is a cardinal sign, which means they want to lead in some area. If the Cancer male cannot lead at home, he will want to be in some type of leadership position at work. This man gets to know you slowly. He wants to do the pursuing, so anyone moving too fast or being too accessible will make him retreat. Instead, send him the message of "I am available…but am I?" A great way to get the Cancer male to chill out and move things along a lot quicker is through his stomach. Make him a really nice meal, and then back off. Maybe text him to say, "I made your favorite dinner. I left it in a bag on my porch. You will have to pick it up and reheat...and oh yeah, I'm out for the night." That will start the wheels turning with questions in his mind, "Does she care? I don't know. She cooked me a meal, but she put it in a to-go bag for me to eat by myself. Hmmm... a confusing mystery to unravel." He begins staking out your house, determined to catch you home so you can share the next meal *together*. And suddenly you notice the crab has taken a small step toward you, instead of all the weaving and bypassing. Unless of course you have given birth to his children. Then he is yours for life.

Cancer Female

A Cancer female has the feminine intuitive energy of the water crab sign. This creates a woman who is a walking emotional mind reader. She can read a room, and you, like a book. The obvious emotions and the undercurrents. Everything. Your feelings literally transfer over to her, and as a cardinal sign, a Cancer woman's first impulse is to solve the problem for you - such as a parent would for a child. This emotional empathy can lead to Cancer attempting to do everything for everyone, reminding me of the Enneagram Type Two of "The Giver". Cancers can overdo or overcompensate to get love or approval. Or expect the opposite in return. But simply put, the Cancer is just looking for someone to love and to get that love back. If you can fulfill that, then you should have a long life together – *if* you have a savings account for your future together. I need to throw in a caveat here: If the Cancer woman wants children, you need to be on board with that plan. Or any plan or business they are pursuing. They need to see you as the solid reliable partner that supports the family and the ideal father for any possible children. If a Cancer female ends up with a partner who is not offering this support, or she sees there are no solid plans – especially financial prospects for security – she will leave rather quickly. This comes at an early point in adulthood where she needs to be thinking about the long-term future. However, if said partner manages to have children *with* her, she is less likely to leave and break up the family unit for those other reasons. Thus, attempting to tolerate an undesirable situation. If her needs are not being met through the partner, she will look to the children to fulfill those for her. Cancer is the mother that doesn't just bake you a cake for your birthday, she makes a castle cake, complete with a moat, bridge, turrets and flags. She goes all out to nurture and provide a loving experience, going above and beyond what other mothers would even attempt. And somehow has the energy to pull it all off.

Long Term love possibilities for Sun in Cancer:

Cancer, Scorpio, Pisces, Leo, Sagittarius. Aquarius too if both parties are on the same spiritual path. Capricorn is a good partner if you overcome the challenges of opposite personalities. Aries is a good match if you both are willing to grow together from and face (accept) your differences. (These sign placements can also be found in a house, or another compatible planet as shown later in this book.)

Mean Astrology - I am driven by emotional needs, my own and others. I lead because I need to.
 If you don't do it my way, you will break my heart. I will manipulate your emotions until you give in, and I get what I want.

- Day: Monday
- Number: 2
- Metal: Silver
- Colors: White, cream, greens, pastels, grays

Cancer Soul Imprint: "I feel to nurture."
Body Rulerships: Uterus, breasts, chest, stomach, rib cage.
Cancer Careers (also look to your Venus sign): History, ancestry, nurse, catering, social worker, real estate, memorabilia, boating, caretakers, chef, designing, mining, plumbers, food service, healing, nutritionist, dietician, sales.

> "Since the beginning
> I have been crying for my mother
> For so long
> That it was my tears
> that filled the rivers
> And I was crying
> When the ocean found its depth
> I have been weeping
> for so long
> That those who know me
> Only know the tear stains
> That scar my face.
> I have known
> The very depths of sadness
> Grief, anger, guilt and pain
> How many times
> Have I crawled back out
> But this time is different."[4]

Moon in Cancer

This is the rulership planet resting in its own sign. The definition of the word "moody" was based on Moon in Cancer. These lunar crabs need emotional expression. If you are weeping, laughing, or in the process of admitting your deepest secrets – this moon sign is happily rushing to your side with open arms ready to listen. They will cry with your torments and traumas and laugh with your triumphs. Grasping hold of your hands and encouraging you to "please continue emoting, thank you very much". They thrive in emotional environments or crumble depending, but psychological entanglements get them out of bed in the morning. And there is no way a mood ring could keep up with their emotional swings. They can cry at the drop of a hat if you hand them a mushy card...or any reason, for that matter. But give it ten seconds and they will be laughing again. Cancer Moon needs to belong – to a family, a tribe, a brood and will makeover all situations into a family structure. They need to feel connected to their heritage and roots. And they never forget a hurt. Moon in Cancer clings to the past in a way that can sometimes be unhealthy or prevents them from adjusting to the present. Many Cancer Moons enjoy physical expressions of love, such as hugs, unless they had a mean Mama. They can be deeply scarred if there was a lack of nurturing in childhood. And you can bet your own relationship with your mother will be analyzed in fine detail to see if there are any remaining "issues" that *you* need to resolve. They are the ultimate "boundary crossers", inserting themselves as quickly into your business as the moon changes signs. But suck it up Buttercup, because this moon sign *cares* and that is more than you can say for most.

Venus in Cancer

These people are aware of all the subtle emotional cues happening around them, and like human barometers surf the waves of mood in the room adjusting to the slightest change. They feel what is going on...what you are thinking. And they love emotional discussions. When it happens, they get a bit giddy, jumping willingly into an emotional melee of feeling frenzy. I love you. No, I love you more! If you are hurt, "Mama will make it better." Or they want you – aka Mama – to bandage their wounds. They love old heirlooms, old habits, old lacy handkerchiefs (washed, of course) and anything sentimental. Sometimes they have trouble letting go of the past and moving on or want things to be like they were "back in the good 'ole days".

In finances, Venus in Cancer may want to control the money flow. They can be good at saving and prefer to gift advice or food instead of handing over cash to those "down on their luck". Cancer is the sign of the breasts and these Venus folks do have a fascination with boobs and chiseled chests.

In romance they enjoy playing roles of dominance and submission. Sex is tied in with the emotions. They can be sweet, sensitive and considerate or intensely passionate. If you hurt their feelings, try making it up to them with a sentimental card or written words from the heart.

Ideal date: Staying at home and cooking a meal together followed by cuddling, talking and sharing feelings, or going to Mom's (yours or theirs - or Grandma's) house for a visit.

Mars in Cancer

These people may seem a bit reserved but don't let them fool you. They are just sizing up the emotional airwaves before reacting. Any action taken is like a game of hide and seek. They alternate between running to hide and coming up in your face to reveal themselves. It's the crab dance. They weave their way around a situation in their very own style of side-to-side. Moods determine their actions. Caring for someone is a motivator and Cancer Mars can fuss and flutter around you like a mother hen or cry on your shoulder like a newborn. They need to beware of the tendency to "smother instead of mother". And they always seem to be fighting an internal battle between the peace and comfort of home and the Mars desire to get on the battlefield..

LEO

*"Leo, Leo, hear them roar
Always entertaining and never a bore
Praise their magnificence and patiently wait
To share their heart, crown and royal estate."*

Leo the loyal lion is a fixed fire sign ruled by the Sun and that means these people were born to shine. Leos are bursting with creativity, ideas and talent, just waiting for an avenue where they can express it. The lion can be reserved or outgoing, but the energy is the same. And they are rarely alone for long. You can bet there is someone in their life that relies on Leo to light up their world. People gravitate to Leo. They want to be in that sphere of sunlight and energy that seems to naturally vibrate off Leo. Lion Suns radiate a level of confidence in themselves that is enviable to those who are insecure. It is not that all Leos have confidence, but there a surety about themselves that always comes across as upper echelon. A strength and a substance. Visualize a lion basking in the Sun in all its glory. A Leo is hard to come up against and take down. They are a fixed sign and will hold their ground, resisting your efforts. All the while smiling that dazzling toothy grin. Like Taurus, they can be physically strong and go head-to-head with a demon with little to no consequences. Many of them own a cat as a pet or at the very least mirror their feline characteristics. Leos demand to be recognized for their magnificence and value. This is where they get a reputation of being susceptible to flattery. It *does* work every time. But they will also be assessing *your* value to *their* life and acting accordingly. Sometimes this strong sense of self-worth can get out of hand and turn into ego. To snare this big cat, you need to shine yourself in some way. Personality, looks, strength...be a complement to them. And give compliments. Complement and compliment. And Leos big heart will soar. Go against them and you will hear their roar...it sounds different in the male and female...

Leo Male

Leo males can tend to be stationary, even though they are a fire sign. He has a "come hither" energy that draws people to him. Like the king on the throne awaiting his subjects to pay homage. And like the cat family, Leo the Lion male takes a lot of naps. They rest for a bit, but when they are ready for action look out. A Leo male can be a joy to be around, until you get under his fur and hear the roar. It is a warning you should take heed of, by exiting the area. This king-of-the-jungle won't hesitate to declare his intentions or give his heart when he has found his queen. Leos want you to look good on their arm – meaning be someone of importance, show that you take care of yourself or be someone of good character that others would respect. You are their royal counterpart, so you need to measure up in the way that Leo needs. The Sun lion is usually in a relationship for the long term. They want compliments and feedback from you. They want your admiration and loyalty. Love is always a grand gesture, even for the shy Leos. So do things up right, remember his special days and give him lots of praise.

Leo Female

Like the male, these women need to know that you value their fabulousness. And they are fabulous. If you aren't showing appreciation (in the way she needs) she will voice her disappointment. Loudly. If nothing improves and she has tried talking with you, but you haven't listened, the silent roar will play out. What do I mean by "silent roar"? She will seek rebellion (rebel lion) in covert ways. Since Leos are typically loyal and don't want to leave the partner or break up the family unit, they may look for a side fling. Someone who can make them feel the love and value they were seeking from you. So, instead of risking losing her, try stroking her ego occasionally or giving in now and then to what she wants? Is that so hard? The situation could easily be turned around. These women are lovable. They love drama. They are intense. These are not flaws. Leos are born to be on a stage. To be entertainers. To shine. So, give them a boost, and you will receive generosity and loyalty in return. I find a lot of Leo females dye their hair blonde or the color of a lion's mane. Some of these felines are terrible with finances and like to spend. If you lack funds, extravagance can be curbed by building up and appreciating her natural childlike wonder and playfulness. Giving health doses of compliments or gifts (many Leo women like gifts) can replace her spending habits. And then take control of the checking account. I have noticed that a lot of Leo women seem to be very prolific in the children department. They do rule the fifth house of children and love affairs. To make this lion purr, work on turning your relationship into a thrilling romance where she is the star of the show, and this woman will be yours forever.

Long Term love possibilities for Sun in Leo:

Leo, Sagittarius, Aries, Cancer, Pisces. Capricorn too if both parties are on the same spiritual path. Aquarius is a good partner if you overcome the challenges of opposite personalities. Scorpio is a good match if you both are willing to grow together from and face (accept) your differences. (These sign placements can also be found in a house, or another compatible planet as shown later in this book.)

Mean Astrology – I lead with my creativity and imagination. I lead because it is my divine right. I follow when I would rather let the assistants do all the work.

I do what I want, because I am royalty.

- Day: Sunday
- Number: 1
- Metal: Gold
- Colors: Gold, brown, yellow, orange

Leo Soul Imprint: "I command honor."
Body Rulerships: Heart, upper back, spinal cord.
Leo Careers (also look to your Venus sign): Actor, romance industry, architect, parenting, designer, event planner, modelling, organizer, marketer, personal trainer, entertainment.

> "No loud roar
> No trumpet blasts
> To let me know
> the lion
> Has arrived at last
> Heralding good things to come

>   Like the Sun ruling his sign
>   Though he hides in Aquarius moon shadows
>   His hallowed arrival
>   Cannot be mistaken
>   For any other
>   would suffer the flaws
>   of society's rules
>   for not one
>   could be so pure
>   So noble
>   So driven
>   So free
>   As he, the light on my path
>   The inspiration
>   The dedication of one
>   who knows the truth
>   and follows it
>   To the letter."[5]

Moon in Leo

These people need all kinds of attention – *yours* – and everyone else's. Leo rules the heart which means this also includes love. They need luxury, and experiences that are "larger than life". Leo is the sign that belongs on the stage, but with Moon here that doesn't mean they necessarily want to be *on* an actual stage broadcasting their private laundry to all and sundry. Sometimes they just want the privacy of their own castle. The Moon represents a parent-child dynamic and Leo has a childlike nature connected to the 5th house of children. This means Moon in Leo can literally act like children at times (endearing or otherwise). Pouting when they are ignored or not getting their way. Then giving you a shiny grin when they are pleased. The solution? Give them your attention, treat them like royalty, play their games and give them some drama. Is that really going to hurt you all that much? They thrive on it, and you just may find that you enjoy the show. Feeling loved fuels that insatiable creative streak streaming through their veins and they will reciprocate big time. When you are an ass, the Leo Lion pride kicks in, but they don't want your pity. They just want to feel something *important*. Like life is important business. Which means *they* are important. They can light up your feelings like the Sun at midday, so treasure their childlike wonder and the gift that Moon in Leo people are.

Venus in Leo

The planet of love is delighted to be in the sign of love affairs and romance. Venus in Leo peeps would love for someone to adore them – preferably bordering on worship - as it makes them feel as if they command all that person's attention. They crave an audience. This Venus placement loves anything flashy as well as grandiose gestures. Many are patrons of the theater and arts or performers themselves. These folks walk with their chin up, head held high and their spine straight, prancing through their domain like the king or queen of the land. They are. These Venus folks take pride in their appearance and want to be proud of their partner as well, so pull up your socks and straighten your collar.

Venus in Leo loves extravagance and are generous with what they have. They love to spend money on the frivolous, seeking enjoyment and are generous to others. This could create problems in finances.

In romance, go big or bust...wait a minute...you forgot about the romance? This is a requisite with this Venus sign. Glamor, glitz and showy signs of love go far with them. Preparing a grand scene works as foreplay, so don't scrimp or get lazy. I know of a Venus in Leo man who attempted to convince a girl to have sex with him on their first date. He said to her...and I quote, "I am going to lay here and allow you to do whatever you want to my body," and he leaned back with his hands clasped behind his royal head, waiting for her to undress him and get to work. Be prepared to make your partner feel powerful in bed. And afterward lay your cheek gingerly on their heart area. It gets them every time.

Ideal date: Getting dressed "to the nines" and going out on the town where Mars in Leo can show you off to friends or the public - even better if you can be photographed together looking fabulous, a trip to an all-inclusive romantic vacation spot or an intimate evening at home where you pull out all the stops.

Mars in Leo

These individuals act with fiery passion when stirred so it is in your best interest not to incite them. They will win. This sign is honorable and defends the helpless, takes pride in their families and are loyal and generous to their brood or partner. They live with purpose and act with authority and courage, which makes them natural born leaders. Leo Mars folk are also attracted to those who are powerful or in leadership positions. They are drawn to the arts. This fiery Mars has a desire to create something, and their hearts are always in their actions (as Leo rules the heart). They do things big in a way that is hard to ignore, and love making dramatic entrances and exits. This Mars can shower you with love, gifts and attention and desire the same in return.

VIRGO

"Virgo with your lines so straight
Could you let them bend and allow fate?
To win your heart I must fit in
With the purity of a soul free from sin."

Virgo. Those precious souls who just want to help. A lot of people find these mutable earth sign virgins hard to get along with, because truth be told they feel they could never measure up to Virgo's standards. And this sign can be exacting, but you need to remember there is a heart underneath all that razor-sharp nitpicking. In all fairness, they are just wanting to find a better way of doing things. As the saying goes, "If you want something done right, get a Virgo to do it." This hard-working earth sign molds the physical reality into something better than it was. And that includes you. Virgo can assess anything or anyone in seconds and make suggestions for improvement. The problem is many of our fragile egos can't handle it. But this analyzing isn't meant to be cruel. It is a way for Virgo to strive for sanity in an insanely chaotic world. Virgos have a strong desire for order. Everything needs to fit nice and snug in its place so that Virgo can relax. They run on mental energy and their nerves can fry with too many things that have no explanation. So, they make up little boxes with categories. And they will fit you into one of them. They *need* you to fit. So, get your ass in there. If you are their partner, you need to fit into that round hole they have labeled "partner". But let's say you are a square shape, not round. No need to worry. Virgo will mold you to fit. Snip off a few of your corners and presto! But that analyzing and organizing can turn to criticizing when Virgie gets frustrated, stressed and unable to solve the problem. They really are just trying to help you, and you aren't following the suggestions for improvement. Their goal? Perfection.

This remaking into perfect plays out in the inner or outer world of Virgo. If it is their inner world, they try to become the perfect person psychologically (Virgo rules the mind) and physically (working out, eating healthy etc.). If it is their outer world, the house and environment will be so immaculate you can eat off the floors. What is interesting is that when they focus on fixing one area, the other usually suffers. They dress like a slob and eat potato chips for dinner, but their books are shelved in alphabetical order by author name. Or they work out daily and count their macros but their house is a hoarder's nightmare. There is a purity about Virgo – and what is reorganized is pure once again. The virginal state. Whether they are inner focused or outer, Virgo hates laziness in others. They are here to work. There is so much to do. How can people just sit and let others do all the work, not lifting a finger? Virgos live to serve. They need to be needed. How noble and admirable is that? So, swallow your pride and take Virgo's painfully detailed advice, because I guarantee all of us could use a bit of fluffing up around the edges. *And* because it makes them happy to help you. *And* while we are at it, get your butt to work. What do Virgos want in return? To hear a "thank you for all you do for me/ the world etc." and an "I love you just as you are, flaws and all." Because Virgo's real secret is that they feel unworthy of your love.

Virgo Male

This man can take what is in his head and bring it into physical reality. He is the earth worker. The perfectionist. Many male Virgos feel inferior or unworthy and give lives of service to others to make up for their seeming lack. They want life to be perfect. They want you to be perfect – and that is dependent on their version of what exactly that is. There is a sense of the untainted, even in the most debauched of these men. Virgo is the Virgin and virginity implies without stain. This makes him strive to be better. He is punctual and may take good care of his environment, having all of his tools lined up just so. And no, the wrench does not hang next to the hammer. Or he may have impeccable hygiene and eating habits.

The earthy sensuality of a male Virgo can be restrained in sex, if he is trying to "get it right" or impress you. Then his motions become almost robotic. Not that he is a saint, but he may wish he was. So, your challenge is to help him loosen up a little bit. He can be modest as he is always aware of his own flaws, but once you have him, this man can be dependable and work hard for the family. His belief system/morals/ethics that he lives by will determine if he sticks around. When he is not working, he is working. Although Virgo males do take time for fun. They love travel, as do all mutable signs, or at least the ability to move around a bit. Since they are so regimented with themselves getting a change of scenery away from work projects gives them an excuse to cut loose. If you have disappointed a male Virgo or not lived up to his expectations, he will be highly critical but means well. If you have a lack of character or basic morals he will be done. He admires someone who works hard and cares for the welfare of others. This is the classic do-gooder, and the world is a better place because of Virgo men.

Virgo Female

These females have organized disciplined minds. They practice until flawless. And they will be the first to tell you they are anything but organized or perfect. They want perfect health, work and relationships. In general, they don't like surprises as it disrupts what they have tried so hard to control or create, and they need planning to avoid problems. The key to this woman's golden heart is to fit into her world. It is ever changing and occupied with thousands of details all revolving around getting something "just so" and being of service to others. There is a lot to do in this world, but Virgo gets hung up on the tiny details. Trying to get them all correctly in a line, and so the to-do list never ends. And they need to finish that list, otherwise panic and anxiety set in. These women need organization of some sort, like you and I need air. They analyze and overanalyze in an attempt to make sure they are getting it right. Everything must have a name and a place. That includes you. These females are independent. Not necessarily because they "don't need no man" (Virgo just corrected my grammar), but because they have too much to do – and getting everything done is paramount to their peace of mind. Work takes all day. Where do they fit you in? Being of service and having a purpose is everything to the Virgoan. So, be part of *that* world. Add to their life. Have genuine pure intentions and a thick skin. This woman will look at you as her next project. Attempting to remold or reshape you into your potential. Try not to take offense. She is probably giving you great advice. Realize that it is herself that she is dissatisfied with, and she most likely berates her own failings in her mind, on the daily. So, let her turn you into a winner. But if she is just nitpicking call her out on it. Gently. This woman needs a kind hand to lift her up and have her back when the going gets rough.

. . .

Long Term love possibilities for Sun in Virgo:

Virgo, Taurus, Capricorn, Libra, Aquarius. Aries too if both parties are on the same spiritual path. Pisces is a good partner if you overcome the challenges of opposite personalities. Gemini is a good match if you both are willing to grow together from and face (accept) your differences. (These sign placements can also be found in a house, or another compatible planet as shown later in this book.)

Mean Astrology – I lead if it will make the work more productive or helps people, and even then, I think I am not doing enough. I follow because I lack confidence, or I am too busy trying to get the busy work done.
　I'm still not doing enough, am I?

- Day: Wednesday
- Number: 5
- Metal: Mercury
- Colors: Glittery, silver and platinum

Virgo Soul Imprint: "I examine for purity."
Body Rulerships: Digestive system, intestines, lower abdomen.
Virgo Careers (also look to your Venus sign): Craftsmen, data analyst, technician, bookkeeper, statistician, secretarial, executive assistant, nutritionist, medicine and alternative medicine, horticulture, seamstress, systems analyst, auditor, home inspections, accountant, writer, spa industry, psychologist, groomers, librarian.

> "Black and white
> You can trust it
> like the words
> on the page
> spelling out
> your logical life
> Orderly and arranged
> Mentally preordained
> Into the framework
> That makes you safe
> Makes you free
> from the worry
> Caused by fools
> who break your rules
> Throwing life off kilter
> Just a little
> Just enough
> To make you run inside
> And hide in the garden
> of black and white shadows"[6]

Moon in Virgo

This is the planet of emotional needs in the sign of service to others. These virgin moons would make great therapists. They can work out your hang-ups and categorize your behavior faster than you can say, "Psychopath." Moon in Virgo feels fulfilled when they have work to do and even more so when they get that work done. They can't relax until everything on the "to-do" list has been completely ticked off – and that means: Every. Single. Thing. Otherwise, that one obnoxious unfinished item can take on a life of its own, morphing into a monster to torment poor moon in Virgo. They lie awake at night, analyzing it from every angle. Beating themselves up for not getting it finished. Counting the hours until the alarm sounds and they can leap from bed to hammer away at it again. The problem is, upon arising another daily list has presented itself and compiled even more work on top of that one irritating incompleted item – that is still refusing to be silenced until Moon in Virgo *finishes it for gawd's sake*. This is how it feels to be inside the head of a Virgo Moon. Completion is a lifeline. It means order has been restored. And they need order. If they run out of projects, there is always you and your life to dismantle and rebuild. Give them your problems to mull over and solve. All the little details that would drive you nuts will truly light up Virgo's world. The Moon is the planet of emotions, and they may listen to *your* gushy ones but that doesn't mean they will join you down the bottomless well of tears. Instead, they will immediately flip into the practical "let's-fix-it" mode. In general Virgo Moons need some type of clean or organized environment to be able to function, whether that is internally (analyzing and reasoning out emotions) or externally (cleaning between the tiles with a toothbrush). So, give them something to work out and solve and they are happy campers logging the numbers and balancing the ledgers.

Venus in Virgo

It's all in the details. These individuals love projects, especially if that includes helping you become a better version of yourself. And they have very specific requirements of their ideal partner. Although even the perfectionistic Virgo realizes their ideal doesn't exist, so they will take you, messy flaws and all. As long as you have some *potential* and no kale stuck between your teeth from that smoothie they forced on you. They willingly jump right into working you over and spiffing you up. These love virgins can be obsessive about "getting it right". A Venus placement here values the healthy, holy, clean or all the above. Pure motives and a pure heart can win them over and help them overlook your bad breath and crusty toenails. Not that Venus in Virgo hasn't noticed your funkiness, but if they discern an innate goodness in your heart, they will tolerate the small stuff. That is - they may not *say* anything, but they just can't resist setting out that bottle of mouthwash and toe fungal cream, can they? (I have noted that a lot of these folks get grossed out by feet or something abnormal to the hooves or toenails, which is interesting as Virgo is opposite to Pisces, the sign that rules the feet.) Your job is to get ahead of the curve and clean up all those tiny spaces that Virgo Venus will be inspecting - the hidden crevices that "catch" little gems. Like a booger hanging from a hair in the nose, and dirt lodged under your fingernails. And for those of you that have an "innie" belly button (hopefully Venus in Virgo *likes* innies), clean that thing out once in a while. In contrast to their spotless souls, you will realize over time that Venus Virgo can be as disgusting as a pig in many ways. It just depends on their rulebook – the one you didn't get a copy of. Work is God to Venus in Virgo, so try not to interrupt them while they are busy earning a living or saving the planet. Or at least ask for a time that you can schedule and interrupt, as they probably don't have breaks or even a lunch hour penciled in. But you can always remind them how *unhealthy* it is to deprive the body and brain of rest and nutrients while handing them a salad. They love it when someone else pitches in to carry the workload while at the same time feeling guilty that they didn't do enough. "If I had worked harder or faster, I would have had time to make my own salad."

In finance, discipline and practicality are second nature to these people. They may get accused of stinginess or being overly frugal, but they worry constantly about not having enough. "I should get the green lettuce since it is ten cents cheaper than the iceberg. But then again the romaine is healthier."

In bed they can be selfless or more concerned about pleasing their partner. Typically, this Venus sign doesn't like surprises (based on other factors in the birth chart) and wants to know what to expect. Routine makes them comfortable, but that doesn't mean they can't be adventurous now and then – just warn them ahead of time. Keep it clean and take a shower first...and oh yeah...leave your socks on. Virgo just washed and sterilized the sheets.

Ideal date: Make sure you have a plan and be on time! Now that we have that out of the way...what to do? Something healthy like working out, eating at a health food restaurant or visiting a farmer's market. Or something with a purpose, such as doling out soup at the homeless shelter. Or educational like a bookstore where you can drop them off at the "how-to" or "self-help" sections.

Mars in Virgo

The planet of passion lands in the sign of purity. These people may have a thousand and one projects going at the same time but there is a method to their madness, so don't interrupt it and by all that is holy, *do not rearrange their workspace.* That haphazard pile of junk on the desk has been specifically organized. And there is so much to do that Mars in Virgo does not have time to reassemble what you seem set on destroying. Mars here has a love of work and accomplishment. They attempt to bring perfection into anything they undertake. They want to do the best job possible and are the ones that always show up when you call for help. The virgin Mars is the Boss Brown-noser and the teacher's pet. Not by choice, but by their willingness to *enjoy* the tedium of work. They are meticulous with details and thrive on having a purpose in life. They may drive you crazy with their constant organizing or complete lack of. But with Mars drive and Virgo's love of duty there is nothing these folks cannot accomplish.

LIBRA

"Libra's beauty of face and flair
Wishing that all in love and war was fair
But no one could ever dispute that you care
When only love was what you fought to share."

Libra the Scales is a cardinal air sign endowed with high intelligence, natural beauty and the creative gifts of Venus. They are represented by the Scales of Justice and are literally the justice warriors of the zodiac. Ever striving for that elusive state of equilibrium and making things fair. These Venus ruled signs want love. Want to express love. Want to find love. Want the world to *be* love. Because with love we will have peace, acceptance and ultimately *balance*. And so, Libras become experts in knowing how to relate with other people. Bending like a pretzel to another's will becomes second nature. Which means they are not necessarily being true to themselves when trying to ensure that everyone is happy (the impossible dream). A lot of times Libra plays a passive role or tells a partner what they want to hear to nail down that ever-evasive slippery state of domestic harmony that forever escapes the Libran's grasp. So, they initiate a silent peace treaty in their heads, with all the rules and details known only to Libra, as they strive to do the work for both parties on keeping the peace. But Libra ends up frustrated and unhappy because the cost for that peace was themselves. You can't do the other person's work for them, especially if your partner doesn't know the rules of the treaty you are trying to enforce. Because of this extreme need to not ruffle any feathers, Libra is the epitome of passive aggressive behavior. They may even argue that they don't argue. But fighting so many head battles to avoid real battles is exhausting and arguing may be a release valve for all the repressed stress. I wish Libra would just open up about their rules. I think we would all gladly follow them. I mean how can you not respect that these noble folks just want things to be fair? And you can trust that this honorable scale sign will always consider both sides and find the one that is just. Which is why many Librans make good lawyers. They are also brilliant with fashion and turning out a good look. A lot of them have dimples and are charmers and social butterflies with many friends. Friendships are gold to Libra and cherished as such. If you know one of these justice warriors, appreciate them for the causes that they support. But look a little closer to see just how genuine that smile is they are trying to pass off on you. Are they faking it for you or for the sake of peace? There's your cue to dig a little deeper and ask about *their* needs. Libra may not have an answer for you right away but continue asking. Teach them that becoming aware of and expressing their own opinions and feelings will not upset the balance of love.

Libra Male

These men are highly intellectual and skilled in many areas. True craftsmen with logical spatial minds or a mechanical mindset with an artistic twist. They tend to dress well. Like the females these men want to share and express love. They seek partnerships and therefore make great life companions, if you give them space to pursue their interests and spend time with friends. Since Libra is a masculine sign, the men express the qualities of this air sign more naturally than the females. They tend to be comfortable in their own skin, relying on Venus charm and probably good looks to get them what they want. In partnerships they are looking for a mirror of themselves. Someone who reflects their ethics, manners and viewpoints. And preferably someone who reflects beauty and refinement mixed with creativity and intellect. They want the perfect partner, but will allow you to be yourself, if your inner character matches their own. Then you can happily bask in each other's company enjoying a life of peace, beauty and harmony. Although they thrive on orchestrating the occasional argument, followed by feigned shock when you suggest that they started it. Libra men are open and reciprocal in their feelings when truly interested in someone. Otherwise, they may tell white lies to keep you from getting angry or to make a good impression. Like other signs there are different types of Libras. One is the oft quoted "Lazy Libra" who relies on charm to get others to do their will, while the other works hard to take care of those they love. The first can be passive aggressive. The second a dependable partner who has your back with some passive aggression thrown in just for fun.

Libra Female

The Libra female wants to express love. Either in her creations she releases to the world, her environment or in relationships with loved ones. She wants to convey herself in an artful way to the outside world to find connection with others or to instigate beauty, change or social justice. Her contributions help her find her place in her community and society as a whole. But sometimes this is at the cost of finding out who she is as an individual. The friends of a Libra female are like family so if she has claimed you, she will be a great friend. Sometimes friends are even more important than family, because Libra *chose* them (choices can be difficult for Libras but are made after a well thought out observation and mental battle – hence any decisions are valuable and worth keeping). They will be reciprocal in romance but also need their partner to be a friend, as well. These Venusians try too hard to please others and this compliance can go on for years. When they get older all that buildup of repressing what *they* want comes crashing to the surface, like a tsunami taking out everything and everyone in its path of frustration and rage. If they are at this stage, get out of the way. Everything you have ever done to them is going to come out all at once, and here you thought the sweet tone and smile meant you two were doing great. The key is to recognize early on when Libra is not being authentic with you. When they are playing the role, they think you want to see, by being agreeable and acquiescing to your needs. Don't let it get to the point of the tsunami, because by then it can be too late for your relationship. Once Libra has decided they are done, that is it. They can be very bitter and stubborn in this regard. Encourage your Libra female to express what she really thinks – you will know she is repressing if there are a lot of arguments. Libras like peace, but they are willing to argue if it will get that balance they are seeking. Both sides need to come to an agreement. But Libra will switch to see your side too, so this can make things confusing. Above all Libra wants life to be fair for everyone, and this is admirable. But the biggest lesson this female needs to learn is that life will not always be what she *deems* as fair, and this insistence can be taken to extreme levels – such as all people need to accept "such and such" or I will take action against you. Libra females have a hard job. It is exhausting to make everyone happy and deliver justice and doing so often means having to break their own code of ethics. An example would be – agreeing with a co-worker who is breaking company rules, but also telling on them to the boss to keep the boss happy as well. Libra will need to learn to cope with any extremist expectations in others and would be better served to keep her own self balanced and happy, and let go the drive to deliver justice to everyone. Narrow the circle of who you go after – meaning go after the ones that are threatening you or your loved ones and leave the rest to their fate. Otherwise, the personal costs to these peaceful souls is not worth the anxiety and the eventual bitterness that follows when fighting too many battles in the name of peace. Eventually they will realize it was all battles and no peace. Instead, dear Libra, channel that need for justice in positive ways. We hate to see you miserable. To sum it up, it is more important for Libra to find balance in herself and *balance* the ways that she seeks balance in the outside world. Happiness begins within and flows out to the world, not the other way around.

Long Term love possibilities for Sun in Libra:

Libra, Gemini, Aquarius, Taurus, Virgo. Pisces too if both parties are on the same spiritual path. Aries is a good partner if you overcome the challenges of opposite personalities. Capricorn is a good match if you both are willing to grow together from and face (accept) your differences. (These sign placements can also be found in a house, or another compatible planet as shown later in this book.)

Mean Astrology – I lead because some injustice is spurring me to take action. I enjoy having followers around me as I am more of an extravert. They make me feel safe and can make the decisions for me if need be.
If you don't do it my way I will passive-aggressive coerce you until you wear out from all my charm and give me what I want.

- Day: Friday
- Number: 6
- Metal: Copper
- Colors: Blue

Libra Soul Imprint: "I mete justice."

Body Rulerships: Ovaries, low back, kidneys, adrenals, skin, lumbar spine, buttocks.

Libra Careers (also look to your Venus sign): Jeweler, cosmetology, human resources, customer service, social or wedding planner, lawyer, investigator, diplomacy, buyer, fashion design, quality control, musician, esthetician.

> "How beautiful is your face
> That an artist
> Could not trace
> The lines
> So elusively
> Sculpted
> Molded
> From the ethers
> Of perfection"[7]

Moon in Libra

This moon sign loves togetherness. Their impossible dream is to see us all unified together in a fair world of like-minded congeniality. And to get this they will look at all sides and are willing to argue both if necessary to get and keep that peace. Moon in Libra needs a partner, and it is as if they have a built-in radar sending out the signal that they are looking for you. This moon is social and wants to share life with someone on a personal level as well. And once they find a partner, lunar Libra will work hard to make them happy. They will come home to a beautiful clean house of smiles. But this moon sign does have a tendency to mooch off of you a bit (all in the name of balancing those Libra scales). Consider it payment for how much work they have to put in to keep the relationship going and make you happy – efforts you are probably oblivious to. Just because Moon in Libra is smiling every time you get home doesn't mean they haven't been busting butt all day to secure your connubial bliss. Chalk it up to a "mooching for tolerating" payment. I mean admit it, you can be super annoying even though Moon in Libra is too nice to say so, and who can blame them for shaving off a few dollars from your savings account? But make you happy they must, as these moon folks can be very dependent on others and are afraid to lose you – always hoping to create that happily-ever-after dream of a wonderful relationship. The word "alone" is not in their vocabulary. Even if avoiding the solitary single life means jumping into a dysfunctional relationship – Libra would rather do that than face the silence of an empty house. They can feel the walls closing in on them and may go knock on the neighbor's door just to get some company. Libra moons make natural lawyers, seeing injustice around every corner that needs to be righted. And did I mention this is one of the most emotionally supportive moons out there? Always making sure they give you a daily dose of romance, understanding and words of support? Remember, these gentle hearts need it in return too, *asshole*.

Venus in Libra

Venus here returns to its own sign of Libra the scales of justice, and Venus in Libra loves when justice has been served. They are ever striving to keep the scales balanced in all areas of life. Libra Venus desires to present a chic elegant look and many have well-proportioned features which create a pleasing appearance. Beauty is balance, baby. This Venus sign will argue for causes if they feel someone is being treated unfairly. But in a relationship, love-planet Libra is willing to do anything to avoid conflict. They love friends and have a very active social life. They thrive at parties and gatherings, sparkling like a diamond amongst the duds. This Venus sign seeks poised and refined interaction and debates. Keep the crass away from their delicate sensibilities.

In finance there may be a lot of dollars spent on esthetic

improvements. Making over their wardrobes, homes and bodies to present a flawless look to the outside world. Financial bank accounts may be shared.

Libra wants everything to be fair – even in the bedroom - so dressing up or playing roles gives set expectations and removes the pressure of trying to be spontaneous while striving for fairness at the same time. Playing a role lets you know the rules ahead of time, so no toes get stepped on or libidos get denied. Venus in Libra is in love with the idea of love and the beauty of its expression. Keep it classy - light and lovely rather than hot and heavy. And if you forget the romance, you have missed the whole point. So, dress up for the occasion, light the candles and set the mood.

Ideal date: A romantic dinner, museum or high-end art show, rubbing shoulders with celebrities, a double date or mingling with their friends

Mars in Libra

These peaceful warriors can internally drive themselves crazy, with Mars pushing for battle and Libra trying to maintain the peace. Mars is ready to act and Libra can't make a decision. Mars in Libra feels the stress of needing to do something and getting caught up in weighing all the sides of *why* they should act. Is it the right time? Is there something I should consider first? Is it being fair to everyone? And if you jump into the mix and try to push them, you will get an argument. Yet they are also the very best at dispelling an argument and mediating. Libra Mars push-pull internal conflict can create a submissive-aggressive way of dealing with others. They are driven to create beauty, balance and justice in the world, no matter how much they have to charm their way into getting it. But you can bet (once the scales of Mars are able to reach a decision) this world will be a much more beautiful place after they get through with it.

SIGNS OF A SOULMATE

SCORPIO

*"A Scorpio dive into levels deep
Where secrets and burdens and emotions weep
For no mere mortal of superficial gleam
Could capture your heart without the highest esteem."*

Scorpio the Phoenix and Eagle is a fixed water sign. Because they are such a mysterious sign and often get a bad rap, I felt they deserved a longer explanation here since so many misunderstand Scorps true nature. Scorpios have the purest love to offer on the zodiac market if you are worthy of it. Which means when considering a relationship with a Scorpio you have a few questions to ask yourself first, such as, "Do I have pure intentions with this relationship?" and "Am I just looking to get something from this person, or am I here because I want to share a deep and loving connection – to give love and share it?" Since most people approach a relationship to get something out of it, are you surprised Scorpio uses their psychic eagle eye to ferret out your shady intentions? Can we blame them for being suspicious of everything when they have the vision and discernment equivalent to their totem bird which can spot the slightest movement of its prey from over a mile away? If you gave the wrong answer to the questions above, it would be wise to move on from Scorpio now, while you can still get out. And be honest about why you are leaving. They will respect your candor. As with all things Scorpio, getting to know this water sign is a complex but highly fascinating and educational experience, so the second thing you will need to determine before getting involved is exactly which type of Scorp you are dealing with. (The low based serpent type - like any other sign - has major flaws and you should move on. They are not a "fit" partner and will usually search for unhealthy outlets such as addictions, cheating etc. to sabotage the relationship.) The average Scorpio type lives in a world of their emotions, and those feelings can be very exacting. You screw me over I get my revenge. They can get trapped in unhealthy obsessions as an outlet for their emotions. Some could sink to bullying if you are treating them badly. If you treat them right however, they smile prettily and carry on an average relationship. The third higher type of Scorpio views the world from a spiritual perspective. These types will only strike with the legendary Scorpio sting if you backed them into a corner with no other choice. And they almost always give you a warning first. They don't want to hurt anyone, but if you give them no choice, they will strike and feel guilty about it later. Scorpios are as loyal as the day is long, sticking by you when the going gets tough. They want you to be loved, happy, healthy and protected. If you find one of these types, hold on to them. A lot of times Scorpions carry the hurt of past relationships where their deep compassion was used against them, but they have so much love to give they stay open for yet another chance to love. The problem is they tend to attract "takers" who mistake compassion for weakness. And these higher type Scorps want love in return, which they often don't get. Or they don't get the time, consideration and attention of someone making an effort to understand their needs. To sum up how Scorpio operates - they are highly logical with a basic nature of emotional intensity. Their choices/actions are almost always emotionally driven. If you stir those boundless feelings – either in a positive or abusive way - that pressure will continue to build inside them unless they find a way to open a valve and let off some steam. If Scorpio loves you, it means they think you are capable of pure love. Every last one of them is looking for their soulmate - a love with shared intensity that fills their yearning to express all of themselves. Scorpio always digs into the deeper meaning behind any discord and will respond with love and forgiveness - forgive but maybe not forget. That would be stupid, right? There's that logic. If you have hurt them, be thankful you get a verbal response. A few words can mean they are willing to talk it out with you. They understand the hurt was accidental. If you get silence then you have hurt them at a deep level, like a knife to the gut. Scorpio needs to get their pain and raging emotions under control before they will be able to respond in a civilized manner to avoid saying something they will regret – so don't push them – unless the fault was theirs. But if the Scorpion totally ghosts you, it is because they couldn't bear the pain of what you did and will not allow you to hurt them again. Sounds exhausting, doesn't it? Now you know how a Scorpio feels and how they love. It's authentic and a bit scary. But hey, if you are a good person who loves and respects the eagle you have nothing to worry about. If that is the case, get ready to enjoy a life with a loyal partner who will defend you to the death, a great sex life, and most importantly the knowledge that you are loved to the core.

Scorpio Man

This man is everything in the description above – a boiling volcano of emotion, but he has a harder time expressing it. The pressure is too much – and any rejection of his love could be too painful, as well. It is why these men often remain single. They channel Scorpio intensity into everything they do, and there is very little that they cannot accomplish through sheer will alone. The Plutonian emotional personality may bottle things up and redirect the intensity into bad behavior or sexual preoccupation. The best thing for a Scorpio man is to become comfortable with his depth of feeling and look for someone who shares the intensity. The problem is, this guy is so used to holding it all in that he becomes, in a sense, unavailable. And so, it follows that he finds "unavailable" females attractive. The one who is "hard to get" gives him a sense of safety from emotional pain. He can pursue at his own pace without fear that the woman would be shadowing his every move or digging into that sensitive interior. A woman doing the pursuing is a turn off. He interprets this as "unattractive" and not a challenge. Again, it is a deep-seated fear that the buried feelings would have to come out with someone "available" and he could get hurt. If he likes her too much, maybe he could be hurt to the point where it would feel impossible to recover. This is one of the least likely men to walk down the aisle, although they still do. And it is many times to a blonde (not sure why this is) who has that essence of the "pure, untouched, virgin princess in her tower" to her. If this is not you, what to do? First determine if he is one of the higher types. If so, and you have genuine intentions and the capacity to love deeply while somehow playing hard to get in the early stages, your chances are very high of capturing this man's delicate heart. What he usually winds up with though, is the ice princess. What he longs for is his soulmate.

Scorpio Woman

This woman is intense, but that is a small price to pay for the love, mystery and excitement she can bring into your life. And note: Water woman will probably need a shoulder to cry on. Guaranteed this girl's undying compassion for others has been abused, used against her or drained her dry by low-level intentioned people that were undeserving of the Eagle's true love. You see, the problem was she dropped her exterior to them – the shell of protection she puts around herself to keep you guessing – and gave them her trust. Her soul. To a *soulless* person. So, "man up" and be that shoulder she needs. Be a *real person*. Listen to her pain when she is hurting. And know that she truly loves you and would sacrifice all to be with you. Count your lucky stars and get over your aversion to emotional effusion. She needs the calm understanding shelter-in-the-storm of your rational yet caring strength to bring her back to balance. It's a trade-off. Scorpio helps you embrace your own emotions, while you help her find calm and stability. Remind her when she is wallowing in her many obsessions that you love her, and everything is alright. Let her know you are her soulmate, the partner that gets her and will be there through thick and thin. Listen to what she needs. Deliver it. But don't be a push-over either. Scorpio needs a strong counterpart because this woman may be weepy (she cries for the world), but she is stronger than steel. Help her get out of the dark places she tends to go when that world is showing her anything but the purity she seeks. Remind her who she really is. And most importantly build trust so this woman can relax for once. Scorpios are not known for being able to take criticism or a joke at their expense unless they trust you. Then they can yuck it up at their own ridiculousness. Otherwise, the laughter is painful to them, and if you are outright mean, look out. They may strike back. Instead, try getting past the claws and find the purring kitten inside that is just waiting for you to come out to play or have a cuddle (and yes, Scorpio will be the first to find sexual innuendos with that sentence.) But truly meet her on the deepest levels of her heart, gently pet this sensitive kitten, give it some milk and you will both be laughing and happy. And once again no sexual puns intended.

Long Term love possibilities for Sun in Scorpio:

Scorpio, Pisces, Cancer, Aries, Sagittarius. Gemini too if both parties are on the same spiritual path. Taurus is a good partner if you overcome the challenges of opposite personalities. Leo is a good match if you both are willing to grow together from and face (accept) your differences. (These sign placements can also be found in a house, or another compatible planet as shown later in this book.)

Mean Astrology – I lead because I follow a deep intuitive sense that tells me the right road to follow. I want real connections with others and won't follow anyone superficial or fake. I follow if I love the person.

I force, because I am obsessing over an emotional need that is putting my rationale out of balance.

- Day: Tuesday
- Number: 9
- Metal: Iron
- Colors: Red, Crimson, Pink

Scorpio Soul Imprint: "I desire depth."

Body Rulerships: Bladder, urethra, genitals, sex organs, reproductive system, excretory system, sweat glands, pelvic bone.

Scorpio Careers (also look to your Venus sign): Psychiatrist, chemist, surgeon, gynecologist, pharmacist, medium, detective, researcher, massage therapist, insurance agent, undertaker, morgue, tax collector, high political office, assistant, psychic, analyst.

> "Passion, will, unstoppable drive
> excite me in ways I know to the
> very core of me
> Intuitively
> we speak
> this secret language of the eyes

> Each understanding in ways
> Indescribable to the spoken word
> But fully heard
> by the soul"[8]

Moon in Scorpio

Why do I FEEL so much? I know of a Scorpio Moon who tried to save a slug that was crossing the doorway in a back storage room at work. She prevented anyone from coming through until she had moved the slug out of the line of foot traffic. Her co-workers continued to tease her forever after by hanging "save the slugs" signs around the workplace. This moon cares for *everything*. But they learn to tone it down a bit for others who just wouldn't understand. Unless it is a slug emergency. If they trust you not to hurt them, they will open up and reward you with refreshing honesty. Their challenge is to master their emotions and not let them rule their every move or decision. This moon sign likes to stay in control to avoid getting hurt. Remember Scorpio feels things deeper than the other signs, so imagine the Moon – the planet of feelings - in the sign of death, renewal and transformations. When their emotions are in upheaval, they can seek and create extreme changes in the world around them. Intense relationships that have value are what excites them. They abhor the shallow, seeing right through your façade as both the Moon and Scorpio lend profoundly accurate psychic ability. These moon natives are not looking for how much is in your bank account, but rather how rich your inner self is. If you are looking for a loyal and devoted friend with a ready box of Kleenex, Moon in Scorpio is a good bet.

Venus in Scorpio

The love planet in the sex sign wants to solve the mysteries of life and death. These people crave extremes and meaningful experiences. At least the extremes make them *feel* something. They seek to unravel any riddle and willingly pull back the fiery curtains of hell to get to the truth. These folks are intense, passionate and committed to whatever incites their interest. Signs that say "forbidden" and "off-limits" do little to dissuade these folks from entering through the creaky door of the haunted house. "Those meddling kids" are always the Venus in Scorpio tribe. This placement prefers a small group of close friends, although people can't help but be drawn to the magnetic undercurrents of alluring Venus and the irresistible pull of seductive Scorpio – this combo is like a double zinger.

Scorpio Venus individuals can be good at making and investing money. They seem to sense trends, ferreting out needed information for where to secure funds. They usually have money because this sign placement is good at hoarding both money and knowledge. Unless they let the desire nature of Scorpio Venus rule their wallet.

For romance, anything taboo gets them out of bed in the morning - or into it – and ready to experiment. But ideally, they want to experience a true connection with someone, and opening their body to all possibilities of sexual expression represents opening themselves fully to the partner on a soul level. They would rather go without sex than have it with someone who could possibly hurt them or where there is no love (unless it has been otherwise agreed that it is just an affair and for amusement purposes only).

Ideal date: Spicy food, a tarot reading, a couple's massage and a hot tub.

Mars in Scorpio

I can already see the fireworks going off inside these people's brains and libidos. This is a sign placement of likely explosions and drastic change. If you stir these people up a revolution could happen. Mars in Scorpio approaches everything and everyone with a certain level of suspicion. They seek the root cause of any underlying secrets. They can have unstoppable willpower and can outlast the best of the best. If their emotions are in it, they will move heaven and earth to accomplish their aims.

SAGITTARIUS

"Sagittarius laughs by day and hides by night
Wrapping their insecurities and locking up tight
Waiting for a heart to see a shared goal
And travel together with a kindred soul."

Sagittarius the archer is a mutable fire sign. That means they have so much energy a dam could burst if it doesn't go somewhere. The problem is they constantly change their mind about where to channel that energy. Yes, they have those pie-in-the-sky goals the archer is famous for, but sometimes Sag gets so distracted they forget to focus on making their dreams happen. All that fire energy forces them to stay on the move. Travel. Anything to burn it off. If they are forced to sit still, they fidget. Sagittarius is restless. And loners at heart, although they secretly long for a companion to pursue their dreams with. If they get hurt too many times, they are happy going it alone. They have standards from a religious or spiritual sense and are usually firmly rooted in some type of belief system by their thirties if not sooner. This is an important quest in the life of a Sun Sag - formulating their spiritual beliefs.

Like other mutable signs when the wind changes direction they change with it. You are either going along with the archer or they are leaving you behind. Sagittarians can be loyal friends and come running when you need them. They are also generous and share what they have - if you can find them, that is. They like to disappear. It is the hermit drive in them that needs to get away for a bit. Many Saggies love horses or at least have an admiration for them. Maybe because their symbol is centaur - half man, half horse? Sagittarius is known for clumsiness. I don't necessarily know if they are clumsier than the next person, but I think any possible lack of grace has to do with having a ton of energy and getting pulled in two opposite directions at the same time. It can make anyone stumble. Sagittarians have busy minds and a busy schedule. Many can retain large amounts of information and are quite knowledgeable and intelligent. Just give them their space. Let them disappear when necessary and they will come back in their carefree Sagittarius way - either the happy bumbling gait, or the run-you-over beeline on their way to the next shining star.

Sagittarius Male

This man has rules and goals for his life. Either you need to be in exact alignment with them, or like most Sagittarians he is just fine being alone. And the brush-off can be swift and painful. Unless you have previously been involved with the Sagittarius man, in which case it is an entirely different story. For some reason they have a hard time letting go of an ex and can often be seen starting a new relationship while still going over and mowing a former flame's lawn every week. They seem to get stuck in the middle of two women like a tug of war where each one pulls on Sag when they need something. Or sometimes male Saggies will date two women simultaneously, unable to let either one go. The Sag male is the epitome of masculine energy. He is proud of his intelligence and will happily spit out large amounts of information from his walking encyclopedia brain on request. If you don't know how to do something, ask Sag. He can usually figure it out. Makes you wonder if he spends his time memorizing instruction manuals.

Male archers can be honest to a fault, even when they don't need to be, yet lie when there is no reason to lie. I have found that many male archers had physically abusive childhoods, often withstanding circumstances many could not endure. Somehow Sag always manages to let it flow off his back, although I am sure the pain is still there deep in the recesses of memory. Perhaps this tolerance of abuse is where his exceptional sense of humor comes from – a coping mechanism. This man has the ability to laugh at even the worst of life. Some Sagittarians are natural comedians that can literally make you crack up in inappropriate settings – like when the priest is giving his sermon. So, if Sag gets arrogant in the know-it-all department or forgets to pick up his socks, cut him some slack. Chances are he has been through an awful lot in life, yet there he is, giving you a laugh, offering his heart and hoping you will share his dreams. Just make sure he cuts ties with the ex.

Sagittarius Female

Getting to know this woman means fighting through the ever-present crowd of people all vying for her love and attention. And this can make it close to impossible to form any type of relationship with her, because she just doesn't have the time. Female Sag is in high demand. And she likes it that way. Most of all Sag females need friends. They love to be surrounded by a posse. And because she has so much energy, she can go, go, go and you will have to keep up if you want her to throw a few crumbs your way. But get there before the others. This is a mutable sign of movement, but if her direction of focus has changed a Sagittarius female can suddenly desire a private space of full-on hermit style living. Like going from one extreme to the other. Which means it is now next to impossible to get to her. This is a sweet fun female who can be really "girly" for a masculine sign, but you will probably see the tomboy side too. Communication is not her forte – meaning communicating clearly what she wants or needs. Often, she doesn't know herself, being continually subject to the demands of others. She wants to please but may do so at her own expense. When overwhelmed, she disappears like the rabbit back into the magician's hat. But if you work a little of your own tricks, she may be coaxed to come out and share her true self with you. And then your whole life becomes magic.

Long Term love possibilities for Sun in Sagittarius:

Sagittarius, Aries, Leo, Cancer, Scorpio. Taurus too if both parties are on the same spiritual path. Gemini is a good partner if you overcome the challenges of opposite personalities. Pisces is a good match if you both are willing to grow together from and face (accept) your differences. (These sign placements can also be found in a house, or another compatible planet as shown later in this book.)

Mean Astrology - I lead because the quest for knowledge drives me. I know more, can retain more, and therefore fall into leadership by proxy. I follow because I enjoy my private time and life, whereas leading can impinge upon that.

In a nutshell – I lead because I am smarter than you. I follow because you have something to teach, or I am afraid to lose.

- Day: Thursday
- Number: 3
- Metal: Tin
- Colors: Purples

Sagittarius Soul Imprint: "I seek principle."

Body Rulerships: Sciatic nerve, liver, hips, thighs, regulates circulation and metabolism.

Sagittarius Careers (also look to your Venus sign): Education, Professor, minister, sales, horse trainer, athlete, foreign relations, instructor, travel agent, broadcaster, commerce, novelists, advertising, life coach, personal trainer, comedian/comedienne.

> "Contemplating
> In my brain
> Ways to keep
> From going insane
> with the thought
> of committing
> To
> You
> To anything
> permanent.
> No restrictions
> No hold
> on my already old
> Reasons to be "free"
> But what is freedom
> Without love
> To free me
> from the chains
> of loneliness?"[9]

Moon in Sagittarius

They have emotional resiliency and bounce back from hurts like a rubber ball. Heavy emotions or reactions make them feel cagey, eyeing for the nearest exit. They would rather be laughing and can tell a mean joke or two just to make sure things stay on the comedy channel. This placement has an interesting dichotomy. The Moon deals with holding on to the past, while Sagittarius is aiming toward the future. These folks have a hard time letting go of old loves and prefer to keep the connection alive – no matter how dysfunctional – to the dismay of their new love interest. They are helpful and generous, but folks with Sag Moon can slide like a slippery snake around blame. It was "not my fault" they loudly declare, meanwhile slinking off to let the other guy take the blame. They like responsibility about as much as they like dramatic emotional displays. They need spontaneity and freedom like the lungs require air and rather than planning out a strategy, they prefer to rely on happy-go-lucky faith that their dreams will come true. That is, if they can keep their bow and arrow aimed at the goal long enough to get there.

Venus in Sagittarius

If you manage to capture a Venus in Sag's heart, they will want to do everything together and share common goals. Be devoted to the relationship and give them their space and freedom (I know it is an oxymoron). Be my everything. Be real, be honest, but don't be too needy or demanding. It can be a great relationship if the love archer would stay put and resist the trigger response to bolt at the slightest sign of clingy. Adventure is the name of the game, and these Venus folks can be up for anything. In this placement, there is a mix of the dignified and refined aristocrat with the "everyday joe" who picks their nose, slobbers and snorts a little when they laugh.

In the finance department, Venus in Sagittarius is a spending combination of loving to acquire beautiful things and blatant irresponsibility. You can already tell these folks' houses are loaded with impulsive purchases that may or may not have broken the bank. Or it could be religious collectibles or piles of books (definitely a need though, not a splurge-buy). This placement would do well to temper their urge to gamble or take risks and use their finely developed brains to acquire a safety net for the future.

Sex is supposed to be fun, not a tedious funeral dirge or the be-all-end-all of life, so don't get so serious on Venus in Sag. Their religious or philosophical views will most likely affect their sexual choices and preferences.

Ideal date: A comedy or horse show, a science exhibit, philosophizing around a bonfire, taking a drive around town or going on a short trip.

Mars in Sagittarius

Once you combine the planet of propulsion Mars and the sign of aspiration and adventure Sagittarius, this placement has an immediate feel of movement. The call of the quest. This Mars Centaur loves aiming for something or having a purpose to their actions. Whether that is to enjoy amusements or chase an ideal, Mars in Sag can't sit still. These individuals do whatever they want. What feels fun right now rather than what needs to be done. They have so many interests going at one time that they may not always finish what they start. And Mars archers may not always show up when they say they will if a far-off starry object distracted them. These people go with the flow and follow the fun. Travel, travel and more travel. The promise of what is over the next hill will forever excite them.

CAPRICORN

"Serious Cappy with manner so stern
Underneath it all you really do yearn
To win your heart I must comport the same
And together we rise to the heights of fame."

Capricorn the fish-goat is an earthy cardinal sign, driven to accomplish in the material realm. With Cappy you are going to get one of two types: The driven workaholic or the victim. These two extremes are caused by a reaction to Saturn, their ruling planet's crackdown-on-joy tendency in their life. Many feel the heavy Saturnian lessons and burdens of karmic payment with the Sun here. A Capricorn will react to the tough taskmaster Saturn by either buckling down and overcoming life's setbacks by working harder than everyone else or giving up and letting everyone know how bad they have it. Cappy has the tenacity to accomplish whatever they set out to do if they are not their own worst enemy. Which one you are with will be obvious. The first you will rarely see as they are always at work, the other will be home lounging on the couch. The workaholic Capricorn wants to rise in stature in the eyes of society. They seek acceptance and measurable representations of their progress and achievements. They want to live up to society's standards and have the "perfect" marriage and family. They will climb the ladder of success until they have reached a trackable marker, whether that be fame, a large salary, title or preferably all. Capricorn is a stern and serious sign. They are not here to jack you around or toy with your emotions in a relationship. They are looking for a long-term stable person who can present themselves well and is willing to take a relationship seriously. But having said that, Capricorns often have an amazing sense of humor and can excel at sarcasm. Most are aiming for goals. They love plotting and planning them out. If you are not there to help them achieve then they will climb over the top of you. The sign is represented as half goat, half fish, so the practical goat side wants to get climbing toward accomplishment in the material world, and the fishy emotional side gives up and wallows in self-pity. Goats climb mountains, and *there is always a mountain* with Capricorn. The gauntlet is tossed to Cappy - either climb the mountain or give up because the task is too daunting. Cappies see mountains where others do not. The sense of reaching any pinnacle represents achieving something others couldn't or wouldn't do. Through this Cap earns their place and right to belong in society. Unfortunately, everything becomes mountains and those of us hanging out on the sidelines can't help but wish Cap would just walk around the Himalayan hurdle instead of insisting that climbing (going the hard way) is the only option. This sign has challenges early in life, but things should get easier as they get older. They tend to loosen up more. If their life has been all work, they reach a point where their former goal no longer suffices. Material achievements are empty. It is at this stage when they could seek spiritual meaning or deeper answers to life. Because the ultimate hill the goat is here to scale is self-knowledge and awareness of their own inner wisdom.

Capricorn Male

If you are in a relationship with this earth sign male, you will get one of the two types mentioned above. The achiever or the victim. Let us just say right now that if it is the latter, you will be financially supporting them and spend a lifetime listening to their woebegone excuses why they can't get off the sofa. Probably this male goat "victim" just managed to level-up and right now would be a terrible time to quit their video game when they are so close to beating their top score. The problem is it will be the same story tomorrow. And victim Cap does like to tell stories. Usually revolving around how they "tried to do such and such, but life just never seems to work out for them". Or they are so good at talking about what they *dream* of doing, that sometimes they start to believe they actually did it. But let's move on to the other type. For the achiever male Cap, work becomes the total focus as it is the means to get them what they think they lack. So, they corral themselves into that cave they call an office, never to be seen or heard from again. You view it as neglect of the relationship while Cappy views working themselves down to the bone as chipping away at overcoming adversity so that you both can have a better life. Only the definition of "better" is entirely Capricorn's definition. The good news is Capricorn males are great long-term relationship material. This tends to be one of the more faithful signs who are open to signing a marriage contract. They want the approval of society which means desiring to be seen as a dependable and solid human being - a committed relationship and family unit is a symbol of that. Man goat-fishies take things seriously, despite their sarcastic or crazy sense of humor. And by the way, the phrase "horny old goat" came from somewhere… If you want to sign up for their life plan, then present yourself as a sure bet for long term. Take them seriously. Take the relationship seriously – the boss or society may be watching, after all. And Cap will be the boss at some point. Make the effort to display an acceptable public image. Male Caps have people to impress and ladders to climb. You are part of that equation, reflecting on the goat as an extension of their taste and choices. But this male will let you pursue your own dreams as well. They want you to contribute to the future of the relationship as much as they do, especially monetarily. Or you can be a housewife if you so desire, just play the role well. Get Cap to open up, laugh and show you a good night out once in a while, and you may just find yourselves enjoying each other's company for many years to come.

Capricorn Female

Capricorn females are workers, no doubt about it, but that doesn't mean this female *wants* to work. Some do, some don't. But they will do what is necessary to achieve what they want or get where they are going. If you assign a Capricorn female to a task they will work hard and shoulder a lot of the burden. They take responsibilities seriously. You can rely on them to be there and get the job done. Capricorns are continually aware of appearances and this female is no different. She always strives to present herself well. Especially if she is climbing the proverbial ladder or mountain to a goal. She thinks people should make themselves *useful*. If you are in her life, you serve a purpose. Otherwise, she has no time for you as life is serious business, and she has aspirations to achieve. This female can work tirelessly to attain the prize – whatever that is to her. If she has focused her time and attention in your direction and deemed you worthy of being her partner, then you can bet she is considering long term. And she will win, so why not just give in to her now? She is a solid bet for the future.

These females find ways to give to you so that you owe them. And they pick when the payment is due. She needs to love you, because Capricorn females can make themselves miserable over time if they commit to someone just for the purpose of moving toward a goal (aka wrong reasons). This woman is very aware of the material world and would rather not be without, thank you very much as she knows what it is like to suffer. So, be clear on what her expectations are, then pull up your bootstraps and get busy securing this woman as your own and building your life together.

Long Term love possibilities for Sun in Capricorn:

Capricorn, Virgo, Taurus, Gemini, Aquarius. Leo too if both parties are on the same spiritual path. Cancer is a good partner if you overcome the challenges of opposite personalities. Libra is a good match if you both are willing to grow together from and face (accept) your differences. (These sign placements can also be found in a house, or another compatible planet as shown later in this book.)

Mean Astrology - I lead because I am willing to work harder than you and make huge sacrifices to achieve greatness.

I also lead because while the rest of you were slacking, I climbed over you on the ladder, stepping on a finger or two along the way.

- Day: Saturday
- Number: 8
- Metal: Lead
- Colors: Black, navy, all dark colors

Capricorn Soul Imprint: "I use strategy."

Body Rulerships: Knees, skin, teeth, joints, bones, connective tissue, nails, hair.

Capricorn Careers (also look to your Venus sign): CEO, business consultant, chiropractor, orthopedic/osteopath, government official, politics, dentist, regional manager, foreman, civil engineer.

"What is there
To lead me on my way
this day of lily pad jumping
With no skill of the frog
To show me the secret
And no turtle to swim beside me
And no leaf to fall gently
And catch my slipping
sliding and careening
off into the dark still waters
waiting to swallow me whole
Strange territory I'm in
A new body, a new home
And new ground to maneuver on
Who is there
To teach me
The ways of the lake
or shall I drown
in the wake
of those speeding by me
Laughing silently
at my inexpert inept agility
with no prior ability to lend
an experienced hand in lily pad land
Sitting still then
And waiting for the calm of the lake
When I can feel the rhythm
of the lily pad
As it flows with the waves
And saves its energy
For standing upright
For I cannot master the steppingstone
Until I have become one with its ways."[10]

Moon in Capricorn

This lunar placement believes that love, just like everything else in life, needs to be earned. Somewhere along the way they have lost their faith and trust in humanity. Combine the hard taskmaster Saturn the ruler of Capricorn with an opposite emotional feeling Moon that represents nurturing. It creates an individual with a twisted view of what it feels like to care and be taken care of. "No worries, money will do that just fine," they say. Money = love. A respected position in society is all part of that picture as well. If you are accepted by the populace or those in important positions, you continue to prosper. These things are safer than love because Moon in Capricorn can control them. And therefore, they are not fond of taking any risks with their finances or their future. They will work hard earning it the old-fashioned way. Or sink into deep depressions because they feel inadequate or incapable of accomplishment. These souls need to acknowledge their own strength and let someone into their hearts and lives for something other than a means to an end, but they view love as the ultimate risk and probably with good reason. Many of these moons have been abused or experienced a childhood devoid of affection. There was always a price for everything. Many of these Cappy Moons do learn to trust later in life. Whimsy, fun and wicked laughter helps lighten their load and open their hearts to love.

Venus in Capricorn

You love a sense of accomplishment. Anything tangible that represents success and symbolizes the efforts you expended to achieve it. Love goats admire status and desire to be powerhouses or big shots. And you love and respect anything that has aged well like a good whiskey or family traditions. To be straightforward, Venus in Capricorn likes wealth, money, power and the things they can buy. They like classic styles in dress with quality fabrics. The material world reflects their own value, so the more expensive an item, the better. They might enjoy age gaps in relationships or playing out roles with parent-child themes. They seek partners for long term potential and public image and will take on the responsibilities of the couple.

In finance, this Venus placement will want to take one of two roles – being the person who completely relies on a partner to provide or being the provider. In the former they seek someone with money. In the latter they seek a complement to their lifestyle. A negative mindset in Venus Caps can cause immobilizing depression. Often these types seek drugs as an escape. Otherwise, there is a willingness to work hard and make the financial savings and investments secure.

In romance, Venus in Capricorn wants to admire you for something. Your ability to be useful, attractive or achieve something in the world is seen as sexy. In bed they are not known to be especially adventurous, preferring constancy over variety. But they can get a bit on the kinky side if they trust you. Overall, they like knowing what to expect so they can accomplish a job well done.

Ideal date: Fine dining, attending a success seminar, or a beer and wine tasting.

Mars in Capricorn

This is one of the best positions for Mars. No other placement is guaranteed to get the job done like these people. Step out of the way or lend a hand, because this lot needs to get where they are going. They are literally powerhouses of productivity and can tackle any challenge. There is a battle going on inside their precious workaholic heads between the Capricorn "we've got a long bumpy road ahead" and Mars "hurry it up" which makes these individuals accomplish at a pace that most can't keep up with. When you combine the two philosophies it could look like "Hurry up and do it now whatever it takes to get it done because we've got a long haul ahead of us to beat the other guy to the pot of gold and more work is piling up by the minute." Say that three times really fast – no commas. Mars Capricorn has already done laps around the track before you can say "tie up your laces". They've got places to go, people to see, competitors to beat and goals to bring into fruition. Unless it is work or progress-related don't waste their energy. They are here to achieve and don't have much time for nonsense. They aren't afraid of the hard work required to get them to their goals. They want real physical tangible results for their labor. They are also Rocks of Gibraltar in a crisis – but make sure it is a real emergency before calling, please, so you don't detract from their projects.

AQUARIUS

"Aquarius adjusting from here to there
Trying to fit everything to which what and where
To enter your organized kingdom I must
Uniquely express and I earn your trust."

Aquarius the Water Bearer is a fixed air sign. Like Scorpio and Virgo, Aquarians are often misunderstood so I will add a little more to the description here for a deeper understanding. Let's start with the two zig-zag lines that symbolize Aquarius which might resemble water but would more accurately be electrical currents running through the air - the brain waves of a mentally oriented air sign. Their ruling planet is Uranus the planet of electricity, thunderbolts of lightning and sudden shocking change. Their water jug pours out new thought onto humanity. In dream symbolism water signifies feelings and emotions and Aquarius carries theirs nicely tucked away from the dangers of life. Yet, Aquarius is often described as a robot in human disguise. This couldn't be further from the truth. Just because they think in future terms and tend to stay in their heads doesn't mean they don't *have* feelings. The truth is Aquarius doesn't *like* emotions. Emotions are messy. Rational thought is much more orderly and comfortable (it terrifies Aquarius to *not know* something). I mean who doesn't like a good drama show as long as it stays on T.V. and not in your own home. And home is an area of sacred space for

Aquarius. If you are going to live with one, be prepared to give over full control of the environment to them. Okay...you can have the basement to decorate...but don't fool yourself. You will catch Aquarius down there too when they thought you weren't looking, "helping" reposition furniture and putting your things away into closets. But they do mean well. Surely you don't want to go nuts having to look at a crooked picture on the wall or an ugly chair? They do it *for your own good*, but really for their own sanity. They can't help themselves.

The truth is Aquarius keeps their thoughts and environment under an iron-clad fist to bury uncomfortable emotions. If their feelings get out, the world spins out of control. Emotions are not reasonable. And it is that very irrationality that drives them over the edge. Most of all, those emotions can *hurt*. And all Aquarians have mushy gooshy centers, no matter what front they are presenting to you. And they aren't going to open that up to just *anybody* – okay maybe to you for a few seconds. The hard shell of control is there for a reason. And seeing an Aquarius overcome with emotion is truly a disturbing sight. If you love them, it makes you want to go out and possibly do violent things to the people who have hurt them. But give them something to laugh about and you will see the water bearer snap out of that messy world of pain and be ready to join you for the next fun adventure – after they redo their sock drawer, that is.

Remember the electricity? Aquarians love to shock or surprise you by being unpredictable. Even in their highly organized world they like to throw a wrench in just for the fun of seeing your reaction. Aquarians like nothing better than hitting the "same ole same ole" with an unexpected blast of lightning just to shake things up. Even they get bored with all that perfection. The Uranus behavior can play out through their actions as well, striving hard to be unpredictable and keep others guessing. But you couldn't ask for a better friend. They will tell you the truth, enlighten you on a few things and get you up to speed with that future waiting just around the corner about to roll in. And they especially love *weird* friends or those who aren't afraid to be unique or different. "Let your freak flag fly", is their motto. Which means Aquarius will accept you, for *you*. They stick through thick and thin because they are a fixed sign. So, give them a little surprise now and then. Just make sure you don't mess up their organization and for the sake of all the saints in heaven, take off your shoes before entering their ashram or newly remodeled hippie van time machine.

Aquarius Male

Male Aquarians are accepting of your quirks. In fact, they embrace them. The weirder the better, in their book. Just as long as it is you being weird, and not them. Then they can sit back and enjoy the show. Weirdness makes you more interesting and gets their minds moving. Throw in a healthy dose of intelligence and it just might be marriage...wait a minute, forget I said that. In romance many of these men like to take it slow and court you for a bit. They want to make sure you fit into their life before they take the sexual step with you. Male water bearers know that getting physical with anyone they are legit interested in, means it will be messy if they need to extricate themselves. So, they will try to stall on any bedroom activity. If you are not on their serious radar, then they can jump into bed faster than a hog chasing a chicken racing to get to the trough. (I will let Aquarius stew on that confusing statement.) However, if they are genuinely interested in you, it can make them nervous to cross that line. Could possibly take forever because sex represents a much scarier level of intimacy. It represents one step closer to their gushy emotional self, locked away with a "no entry" sign on the door. And attachment brings the potential to hurt them. But if it is casual from the beginning – hey no hurt feelings, honey. It was just sex. They can be as cold and unfeeling as their robot reputations. At least they are honest about it. They are not usually oversexed as a rule, preferring mental stimulation. I am quoting an Aquarian male here, "Sex every day is a chore. Sex every two weeks is fun." A lot of these males tend to be bachelors and hold out longer than most before settling down. They hate following the norm and prefer to set their own rules and standards, but if you follow those "rules" they might consider being faithful.

Which brings us to their work life. As I said male Aquarians tend to go against conventions in expected gender roles. Such as a male being expected to support the family financially. They resent being seen as the bread winner and will sometimes choose a low paying job just to rebel against the stereotype, whether they are aware of the reason or not. And they are rebels (men and women alike). It also satisfies their need for being unpredictable, but ultimately it could be in their best interest to toss out those excuses if they hope to financially secure their future. But for those of you that are already well off on your own, this male can be a refreshing partner who lifts your spirit and boosts your goals. Just don't expect sappy emotional reciprocation every day. Or ever unless there is a water moon sign or house involved.

Aquarius Female

This woman is the supermom - the woman who can do it all. And she does. She is the queen of her castle so don't even think you are going to mess up her vibe or space. Her one lesson in this life is to learn to rely more on her intuition. There are a lot of female Aquarians that rely solely on knowledge, and it only takes them so far. This could be their Achilles Heel – I mean come on, no one can know *everything*. When they combine intuition, they are unstoppable. She was born to be an entrepreneur whether she chooses to work for herself or not. Aquarius females thrive in an environment with little to no supervision. They love having the freedom to move about and make their own choices and decisions. If you are into traditional roles you can forget about it with this female. She is a free bird, so you better accept and like it or shove it where the sun doesn't shine. But just because she likes freedom doesn't mean she has any intention of leaving you. The Aquarian female is still a fixed sign which means loyalty, but she wants to make sure she can spread her wings and fly if the mood strikes her. If this woman loves you, that is it. She will stick with your shoddy ass through thick and thin. The Aquarius water bearer is a partner to be proud of and show off to others. Being a people person and a friend to the world it is hard not to love this female. And guys get ready for a woman who can rationalize. If she also lets you into her tender heart and feelings, then consider yourself a lottery winner. You have probably died and gone to heaven.

Long Term love possibilities for Sun in Aquarius:

Aquarius, Gemini, Libra, Virgo, Capricorn. Cancer too if both parties are on the same spiritual path. Leo is a good partner if you overcome the challenges of opposite personalities. Taurus is a good match if you both are willing to grow together from and face (accept) your differences. (These sign placements can also be found in a house, or another compatible planet as shown later in this book.)

Mean Astrology - I lead because I think of what is good for the whole, not the individual.
But really, I just do what I want, because staying unpredictable makes me feel different and special.

- Day: Wednesday
- Number: 4
- Metal: Crystal
- Colors: neon colors, bright blue

Aquarius Soul Imprint: "I know to know."
Body Rulerships: Ankles, calves, shins, circulation of blood
Aquarius Careers (also look to your Venus sign): Electrician, electronics, electrical engineering, technician, astrologer, judge, activist, fundraiser, pilot, mechanic, physicist, computer repair, metaphysics, phone service, car sales.

"Take me into the altered states
of your consciousness
webbing and wrapping around me
Like a maze of mysteries
theories and discoveries
Always challenging
Always awakening
Making me think of new ways
of viewing things
through your eyes
walking in your shoes
Tasting with your tongue
Feeling with your arms
Dreaming in your soul
Turning my existence upside down
Taking me into new lands
of reason and rhyme
where each day is a new idea
a new concept, a new way
a new you, a new me
Opening me up to
the discovery of

life beyond life
time beyond time
and experiences unknown to me
prior to knowing
your beautiful wonderful weird self
An elf
leading me to the fairy land
Invisible to me
only hours before encountering you."[11]

Moon in Aquarius

These people need - and attract - a lot of friends, probably because they are so emotionally balanced. To the degree of *no* emotion sometimes. Some people see them as too robotic, having little to no care for the sensitivities of others. While others consider Moon in Aquarius people a safe haven of cold hard logic to run to when the going gets rough and the feelings get overwhelming. Trust these folks to always have a nice rational response at the ready. Nothing like a bucket of ice water reality to snap you out of the doldrums of feeling sorry for yourself. But they "let you be", and fight for equality, and will expect the same treatment in return. They love their space and having control of it. Unpredictability is a requirement and exposure to weirdness a balm for their soul. Probably because it helps diminish their own feelings of "being different". They know they can't fit in, so why fight it? Then they drive you bonkers hammering you over the head with their uniqueness. The good news is, if you are weird too, you are welcomed. Those bizarre bohemian woo-woo types that ride in with a message from your dead grandmother find an open door in the Aquarius Moon abode. So let these inventive heads that rule the heart do it their own way as they create a better world for the rest of us tomorrow.

. . .

Venus in Aquarius

This Venus placement loves the bizarre. The odd, the puzzling, the radical and the revolutionary. They want peace, progress and change for the good of humanity. They prefer to work in groups for the bigger picture rather than on a more personalized one-to-one basis which is too intimate and makes this moon sign concerned about neglecting all those *other* people. Venus in Aquarius makes friends quicker than I can come up with a clever metaphor. Abstract art might appeal to them as well as unusual job descriptions and unique viewpoints. Venus in Aquarius loves a level of eccentricity in their partners. The predictable is so booooring. These people may be more inclined to unconventional relationships or roles. They want to be friends with their lovers and admire smart forward-thinking people like themselves. The relationship will be based on their rules or ideas of how it should be conducted. Even so, they love surprises and spontaneity providing it fits into their realm of what is acceptable.

In finance, these folks would rather concern themselves with more high-minded issues but do save up for the occasional rough patch. And with cash they are more conventional than they think.

Sex without attachment is a great turn on, because with attachment comes all those messy emotions. Thinking about it is a lot safer and preferable to actually *doing* it. And distance definitely makes the heart grow fonder. The more you detach, the more this individualistic Venus wants you.

Ideal date: Live music or a concert of their favorite beatnik band, a humanitarian fundraiser, a science convention or a museum.

Mars in Aquarius

They love to show up on their own terms, in their own time and not necessarily dressed for the occasion. These are the rebels with a different cause. They use craftiness and willpower to get their way. But they give others their space and the freedom to be who they are as individuals. The fiery energy of Mars is channeled into intellectual or humanitarian pursuits and causes. They must do things in their own way, and they don't comply easily, so step aside.

PISCES

"Pisces as wise as the first dawn of time
Cannot contain all of you in just one rhyme
To win your heart and soul, the pair
I must be the ever-most uttermost of the rare."

Pisces the fish is a mutable water sign that embodies all the others. They can literally be whatever they set their minds to becoming. Pisces is the chameleon of the zodiac, often taking on different "roles" depending on who they are talking with, to *merge* better with others. They can be whatever *you* want them to be, as well. But as you can guess, this role playing can be exhausting. So does comforting all the many dear souls that want to cry on this bleeding heart's shoulder. And the line grows ever longer, life's tortured travelers awaiting their turn for a piece of Pisces advice or understanding. It begins to put the fish in a position where they will have to start sacrificing their own needs to help all these desperate charity cases. It is at this stage you will notice the fishy wishy getting wishy-washy and becoming hard to pin down. And before you know it, they disappear. Diving deep into the murky ocean depths where you will never find them, much less dare to follow. This is their vacation from the woes of a cruel world to get a recharge. Some fish choose to escape by more detrimental means such as using addictive substances. It is important for Pisces to choose a healthy way of getting away from it all, and it would be wise for them to work on establishing stronger boundaries. But then, I am not telling them something they don't already know. They have 'been there done that' in all areas of life. It's why they are in such high demand.

Pisces literally needs regular retreats to nurture the right-brain dreamer and shut out the left-brain world for a bit. When Pisces resurfaces, they are all smiles again and ready to take on your challenges. But should they be permitting this endless cycle all the time? Just because they are mutable and can roll with the punches, doesn't mean they should be guilted into handing out words of wisdom and patting your shoulder every time you corner them with every horrible humiliation that has ever happened to you. It starts to become glaringly apparent that being sensitive and caring deeply about the welfare of others could become a handicap. Over time Pisces gets sick of it and prefers to share that compassion with children and animals where there is at least a little reciprocal reward on the other end. They are the gentle dreamers, who learn quickly to toughen up to survive in today's world. I just hope these wise fish Suns don't ever let go of their imagination and ability to dream. And they are all super psychic by the way, reading minds is second nature so that sly smile means "they already know" - your thoughts and intentions - even better than you.

Pisces Male

A male Pisces has a tender heart, even though you may not see it, you hear about it. That pumping pile of cardio marshmallow is sometimes hidden under a "tough" exterior. This is a survival mechanism. They show their "game face" so they don't get hurt. I can hear the male Pisces' eye rolls right now, but come on, we know it's true. The symbol for Pisces is two fish swimming in opposite directions. This means there are always two directions this man can go. Which will it be? Two internal choices in everything he undertakes. And two consciences. The good fish whispering, "You probably shouldn't do this," and the bad fish snickering, "Do it." If you are dating a male Pisces mutable sign it helps to think of him as a sailboat that needs wind to let it know which direction to move. Once the breeze hits, Pisces is off and running. And you know how hard it is to sail against the wind. So, you are either going with him, or he is already long gone. The trick is to *be* that wind. While he is tacking and trying to catch a breeze, give him a direction and lead the way. Play hard to get and hard to please. It will spur him on to double down and try harder. Don't be a pushover. Make him work for it. Once Pisces' sails have caught the gales there is no stopping him. He can achieve anything he sets his mind to – all it took was a little motivation from you the cruise director. Together you can journey into the sunset accomplishing happy dreams.

Pisces Female

Pisces women are idealists, donning the rose-colored glasses of their ruling planet Neptune – which helps them see the fairies better. And don't tell Pisces those things are old fish tales. The world is a magical place to these mermaids, and they can see on levels you never dreamed existed. And to say these women are psychic is an understatement, which means they know exactly what game you are playing. They are already light years ahead. Be kind to this siren if you want to attract her, but don't be a pushover. Chances are it is going to be *her* attracting *you*, but I digress. Have a spine, otherwise she will twist and manipulate you ten ways to Sunday into believing whatever she wants. Pisces women need to take care to find time away from the daily grind. Away from people for that matter. They are psychic sponges that absorb every emotion in their proximity and need space to clear their energy field. They can also get so drained from carrying everyone else's load that they are prone to unhealthy choices when seeking an escape mechanism. These females are often called on to be emotionally mature before their time and can be put into positions at a young age where they need to stand up for others. Now that Pisces is an adult, she should give herself permission to dream and find the magic of childhood again that lives in her soul. Love her for that soul, and Pisces is happy to share her enchanting inner world with you.

Long Term love possibilities for Sun in Pisces:

Pisces, Cancer, Scorpio, Aries, Leo. Libra too if both parties are on the same spiritual path. Virgo is a good partner if you overcome the challenges of opposite personalities. Sagittarius is a good match if you both are willing to grow together from and face (accept) your differences. (These sign placements can also be found in a house, or another compatible planet as shown later in this book.)

Mean Astrology - I lead when I am sure I am right about something, and the information will help a larger pool of people. I follow because I am disappointed in the world and lacking inspiration.

I lead because only I have the true answers. All others are wrong.

- Day: Friday

- Number: 7
- Metal: Tin
- Colors: Green, white, cream, gray

Pisces Soul Imprint: "I believe in belief."
Body Rulerships: Feet, toes, lymphatic, meridians, spleen.
Pisces Careers (also look to your Venus sign): Dancer, entrepreneur, PhD, fisherman, coast guard, boat captain, finance, psychic, bartender, addictions counselor, jail warden, hospital administrator, religious vocations, lifeguard, painter, sculptor, film industry, caretaker, marine biologist, pharmaceutical.

"You say all your faith is lost
in fairy tales and things
Your dreams
Have escaped you
Left you dying
in the ashes of another
whose words robbed you
whose games maimed you
Renamed you
Into an unbeliever
In the truth all around you
Waiting for you to
pick the flower
And catch the elf
Hiding beneath its petals
Hidden to the eyes
of the realist
The idealist
Believing there is no
such thing as flying
without wings
Singing without a song

Believing only in the wrong
Can I show you instead
A rainbow I hid
in a box
underneath my bed"[12]

Moon in Pisces

These are the sweethearts of the zodiac. Other people can immediately tell, from the sad look in the eyes, that this moon sign cares. These psychic souls carry the weight of the world's troubles on their shoulders. They feel everyone's pain and have already walked a mile in your shoes. If not in actual life, then by the direct osmosis of your feelings. But keep in mind those ocean deep emotions will rule them and their daily decisions, as well as a razor-sharp intuition. They are most likely reading your mind as we speak. This can sometimes tempt the Pisces to cheat, knowing they can manipulate the situation. Pisces Moon needs to know what the feeling or vibe is, to gain valuable information on how to proceed. Co-dependents, cling-ons and those who would take advantage are drawn to this moon as if by a homing signal - zeroing in on any available ear to listen to their sorrows. Pisces becomes the dumping ground for their burdens. Maybe that is why these lunar fish people are so hard to pin down. Like trying to grab a slippery oiled eel before it dives beneath the waves. Their notorious disappearing acts could be a much-needed defense system against these manipulators. But treat them with kindness and respect and you will get that in return, along with genuine love and a friend for life.

Venus in Pisces

Does anyone really understand Pisces, much less know what the fish really wants from us? For a sign that embodies all the signs, they may not know either. With Venus here, we witness your soft spot for the unfortunate and every downtrodden underdog that begs for a biscuit. That much is evident, but what is going on in that mermaid/merman heart of yours? Venus in Pisces values love – unconditional, unrequited or any type – and make it intense, reactive or romantic, with preferably a fairy-tale ending. When you meet them, let it slip that destiny was what led you to their doorstep and they get all starry-eyed. They like to dream about love, fantasize and can be great visionaries of the future. Venus in Pisces may take you on a romantic date and seem to have orbs only for you…that is until their phone starts ringing with calls from the "victims in need" hotline. Or you pass that sweet homeless kitten on the way into the restaurant that Mars in Pisces rushed off to find a home for. Even if they tell you they don't like animals, you can bet they are still secretly thinking about how "kitty" is faring.

Finance – Love fish aren't interested in money for its own sake, but rather what it can do for them. Pisces could be careless with it, or when motivated be as rich as King Midas. Their choice.

In romance these dreamy souls want the ideal. A fantasy come true – so find out what theirs is. Venus in Pisces, like Venus in Sagittarius, may bring religious beliefs into the bedroom. But in general, they are very open and willing to experiment, often changing their preferences on a whim from day to day. Don't be surprised if they show up in a role-play costume.

Ideal date: A psychic reading, a trip to the ocean or anywhere near water, boating, visiting an aquarium or going dancing.

Mars in Pisces

Mars in Pisces loves alternating between playing victim or being the martyr. This fiery fish placement (not to be confused with fried fish) frequently acts on feelings, intuition, instinct and whims, so prepare yourself. They can prefer to go with the flow, dousing Mars energy with a bucket of water if it gets too insistent on direct action. They look for the magic however they can find it. This placement loves escapes from the drudgery and the pressures of ordinary life and rides rough waters finding their way when others get lost at sea. And when they set their mind to it, there is nothing these sea nymph warriors cannot do.

CHAPTER 4
Elements & Qualities

Your astrology chart is like owning a gold mine, rich with veins of information. You can discover your life path laid out in all its components if you can learn to decipher the code. I am going to go a little deeper into the basics of astrology to familiarize you with a bit more before we get into the actual soulmate placements you will be looking for on the Soulmate Quiz. First, let's talk about each sign's elements and qualities. It is helpful to learn these, because even if you forget the characteristics of the signs, if you remember the four elements and/or the three qualities, you know something about every sign.

FOUR ZODIAC SIGN ELEMENTS

Each of the twelve signs belongs to an element. There are four elements – fire, earth, air and water. This means that there will be three signs in each element. Elements give commonalities in personality, and two signs that share the same element take on the same attributes, making them naturally congenial with each other. Each element contains a capacity for emotion and the style in which the individual expresses that emotion. If you both share the same emotive style, you are more likely to understand each other and get along. For enduring romantic relationships, each element goes best with their own – fire with fire, earth with earth, air with air and water with water. I have also found that in long-term relationships, fire also goes naturally with water and earth goes naturally with air. Fire and water are more intuitive and feelings oriented, while earth and air tend to be more practical and logical. In soulmate placements, the elements provide valuable information and form key relationships between the signs.

Using the following chart, write down both you and your partner's elements. (If you do not have compatible elements, do not despair. There are many possibilities for soul mates, not just Sun sign elements, as you will see later in the book.)

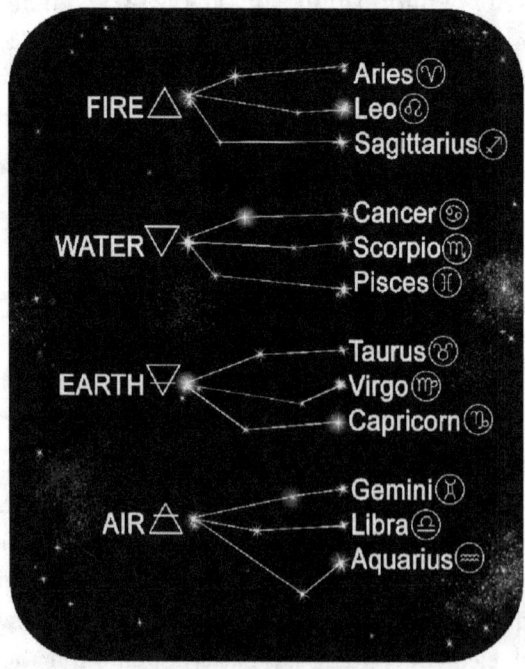

Figure 8 - Signs and Elements

The compatible elements are:

- Fire with Fire
- Earth with Earth
- Air with Air
- Water with Water
- Fire with Water
- Earth with Air.

Fire – A fire element personality is just like it sounds – fiery. They are usually outgoing extroverts, energetic, and their overall style is formative and creative. Fire can simmer, burn raging hot or fizzle out. They value artistic or inspired creative expression

Water – The water element is the feeling personality and because of this they can shy away from others or be introverted. Water is fluid, and its nature ranges from heavy and still to active and flowing to explosive force. Water types value intuitive and emotional responses and are concerned with issues of love.

Earth – Earth types are producers of the tangible. They focus their attention within the realm of the material world. The nature is firm to unmovable to unstable. They value physical results and "real" evidence.

. . .

Air – Air elements are the thinkers. They breathe in the realm of lofty thoughts and cerebral deduction. They can often be extroverts. The nature is detached to focused to psychosis. They value the intellect and rational perception.

Keep in mind the following compatibilities between elements is a general overview and may not determine whether you can bond or not bond with a particular element.

A fire sign with a fire sign – If you bring two fire signs together, we may need to get out the fire hose when this pair starts to heat up. Together they could set a forest ablaze with their passion. Sparks ignite in a millisecond and rage out of control as fire with fire can be prone to a good old-fashioned brawl now and then. They secretly find sparring exciting. And all that gasoline added to the flames just creates more of a challenge. They make quick work of foreplay. Fire with fire can use all that combustion to either fight, or fuel each other's dreams.

A fire sign with an air sign – This is a great combination because the air sign gives the fire sign energy to burn. But the fire can take air for granted, using up their precious reserves and always requiring more. And fire can get frustrated with the lack of an impassioned or more demonstrative response from air. Both will be stubborn about getting their way but enjoy long conversations that can run the gamut from stimulating to just a lot of hot air. It will have to be a mutual choice of give and take with a dash of humbleness to make this work.

A fire sign with an earth sign – This pair can get along well together if the earth sign doesn't bog down or bore the fire sign until the passion dries up, or the fire doesn't drain earth of its resources. Although both have a lot of stamina and energy for going the distance. Fire signs can seem impractical to the ever-steady earth and earth can be a stodgy stick-in-the-mud when fire wants to run free. But they can make great things happen in the world of earthy things with creative fiery ideas. A careful balance will be needed.

A fire sign with a water sign – These two can create sweet love together or blow up like a volcano of destruction, so step out of the way if you sense the tension building. Who will get hurt is the question, as fire and water are evenly matched? But most of the time this is an excellent pairing of friends or lovers who "get" each other. When water meets fire, we have either a sexy hot tub scenario, or a nice cup of hot tea. They alternate between both. Once settled in, they happily steam along to their own song going places none of us ever dreamed possible.

An air sign with an air sign – Will these two ever stop talking? Maybe once they start the blinking and winking and getting all lovey-dovey with the eyes. I mean geez. These free-flying friends turned lovers can look so cute together the rest of us do an eyeroll. They love sharing their wily wit, distant dreams, and long-winded thoughts about a lengthy life together. Hopefully these two are "in it to win it", because well, *we just want them to*. But there will be all hell to pay if one gets selfish and neglects the needs of the other. Then the frosty winds blow, and the world freezes over.

An air sign with an earth sign – Will these two ever meet? Let's hope so because they would get along famously. Earth counting the numbers in the checkbook while air is expounding on the state of the world. Earth makes air's lofty world ideals happen with practical follow-through and air gives earth a reason to keep chiseling away in the mine. These two elements understand each other and rarely ruffle each other's feathers, at least not deliberately. But the ruffling happens on its own at times when the stubbornness in both elements fight for ground.

An air sign with a water sign – These work well together if the water sign doesn't get too soppy and drippy and slushy and weigh poor trapped air sign down with drawn-out dramas of emotional woe. And if air sign doesn't blow their sometimes harsh, cold wind of indifference and freeze over the sensitive water heart. Air likes to stir up the water sign's emotions – only the fun feelings of course – because water theatrics are entertaining, meanwhile the water sign gets great advice from these intellectual brainiacs.

An earth sign with an earth sign – Was there ever a more accurate definition of a "sure thing"? Like two rocks sitting in a field, earth and earth stick together side by side. Unmovable against the winds of time weathering their stony faces. Their love still spanning the ages. Standing strong against the harsh elements that would wear down another pairing. It is usually outside forces that shake these two apart or threaten their foundations. Together they build an earthy edifice empire of a legacy that lasts, or they experience a tragedy of loss through greed or foolishness.

An earth sign with a water sign – These two seem to go together like rain cradled in a muddy puddle. Earth is nourished by the love and emotion from water, and water gets grounded and stabilized by earth's no-nonsense approach. They are very different and sometimes do better taking each other in small doses. Earth and water also seem to polarize to the needs of one or the other. Either its earth's way or water's way, which means one has to give in and go without their needs being met. Earth will give material security, but water wants the emotional and vice versa.

A water sign with a water sign – What are those two merpeople talking about, sitting on an outcropping of rock miles from shore? We can't hear the conversation, because only a water sign would understand. And a merperson always guards the secret that the seas were once formed by the salty tears of water signs. This pair does one of two things: they swim happily together weaving seaweed into their hair and sharing an ocean of emotion in their hearts or they drown each other in the murky depths of despair. The understanding can be deep but who is going to lure them back to shore to take part in the real world?

WHAT'S YOUR MODE-US OPERANDI?

In addition to elements, I mentioned qualities. And each sign has one. "Quality" is short for "quadruplicity" or "modality" (modes). Calling them "quads" and "modes" is more fun, so I'll do both. There are three modes, which means there will be four signs sharing each. They are called cardinal, fixed and mutable. Where elements are characteristics, quads are ways that particular signs take action. If you are in an incompatible element, oftentimes a mode will help bond you together, even though it is important to note that the signs sharing a quad are squared to each other (see Chapter 2 under aspects).

Determining your mode or quad is not necessary for identifying a soulmate, but it is helpful in understanding yourself, the dynamics between two people and how those play out in relationships. Who will be the leader, and who the follower? Who is dominant or assertive and who is passive or receptive?

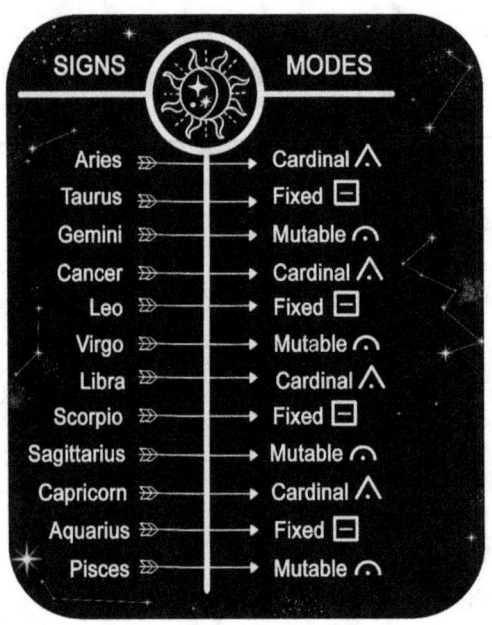

Cardinal: Cardinal is a natural born leader. Cardinal signs are known for being initiators and originators. They are pioneers that show the way. Cardinal signs give the driver of the train directions to where the train is headed, and everyone else needs to get in their seats for the ride. If need be, the cardinal sign will drive the train his/herself if necessary. In fact, they usually prefer to be in the driver's seat. Get on board. The train is pulling out. Cardinal could be viewed as the owner of the railroad or the Locomotive Engineer – driver of the train.

. . .

Fixed: Fixed is a supporter or follower. The characteristics of a fixed sign are steady as she goes, reliable and constant, maintaining what has already been created. They are happy to let someone else lead or give them direction. Sometimes they will take the lead if need be but either way they will make sure everything gets done so everyone can get where they are going. Once fixed understands the goal, they can work tirelessly toward it. Fixed signs would be considered the Conductor of the train, who manages the activities of the crew and passengers and makes sure everything continues to run smoothly. They sell and collect tickets and keep the train going.

Mutable: Mutable is both a follower and a leader. The characteristics of a mutable sign are changeable and flexible – they can be either cardinal or fixed. They decide which based on circumstances and motivation. They are fine with being the Engineer or the Conductor. However, if the mutable person loses interest in the current direction or path, they can suddenly decide to switch to another railway track or stop the train altogether. This can throw a cardinal or fixed sign for a loop, as the mutable person now completely changes the agreed upon destination.

If two cardinals get together – Using the analogy above, you can see that it might be a good thing if both have a similar trajectory or unified life goals because they would be sharing the same train. But if they are going in different directions, they may never cross paths. Or one will have to give up what they want in favor of the other's desires. If they can come to an agreement or compromise, they can enjoy pursuing a common objective together.

If two fixed get together – Like two cardinal signs, they will need similar values and goals that work in harmony together. Two fixed signs will have to mutually decide what is the important goal and honor each other's dreams, knowing they can stick it out together. They rest in the confidence that each can depend on the other, to be there and show up - two rocks of support. If everything lines up, they are in it for the long haul.

If two mutables get together – They will do best when designating ahead of time who will do the leading and who will do the supporting. Ideally each get to play both roles in some way. For example, one will be the leader in charge of what happens with the home life and children (cardinal) and keeping the household running (fixed). The other is in charge of the finances. They earn income and decide the budget (cardinal), but also show up to work every day and pay the bills (fixed). Problems arise when these two have no clear-cut direction or division of tasks. They drift along and could eventually drift apart.

If a fixed and a cardinal get together - The cardinal ideas always lead the show. They are the instigator person. The goal-setter. They hold the vision for the relationship. The fixed person assists and carries on the day-to-day details to ensure the longevity and/or completion of the shared vision. Seeing that the fixed sign honors their need to pursue a certain life direction, the cardinal sign can be very supportive in return, giving the fixed sign room to achieve their dreams as well. The cardinal sign may offer ideas, connections and energy to make that happen. They part when the cardinal tries to dominate.

If a mutable and a cardinal get together – This will work best if the mutable is already in agreement with and excited about the direction the cardinal wants to go. They will need cardinal to motivate or sell it to them if they are not already on board.

Mutable will then happily assist with the common goal by standing side by side and leading the charge or being the person who consistently carries out the details. But if the cardinal is stubborn or bores the mutable, thinking only about themselves, the mutable is out of there. On the flip side, be wishy-washy with the cardinal sign and they leave you in the dust.

If a mutable and a fixed get together – This works best if the mutable has decided that they want to be in the relationship long term. Just wanting an adventure or enjoying shaking things up just for entertainment's sake can cause the fixed sign stress. Mutable needs to realize the value of the fixed sign's loyalty. The fixed sign will need to be a bit more flexible if mutable wants to quickly change directions or be willing take the lead and give motivation if mutable is losing their way. Otherwise, the mutable will carve out the relationship's life direction and goals and the fixed sign will be the backbone that gets it all done.

RULING PLANETS

You can also decipher a sign's characteristics by looking at its ruling planet. It is a good idea to become familiar with the ruling planet of your Sun Sign for added depth and information about the sign. For example, you may have your Sun in Taurus with its ruling planet Venus. Wherever Venus is in your chart will also be a hotspot for insight. Also notice any prominent planets in your chart, and their respective signs.

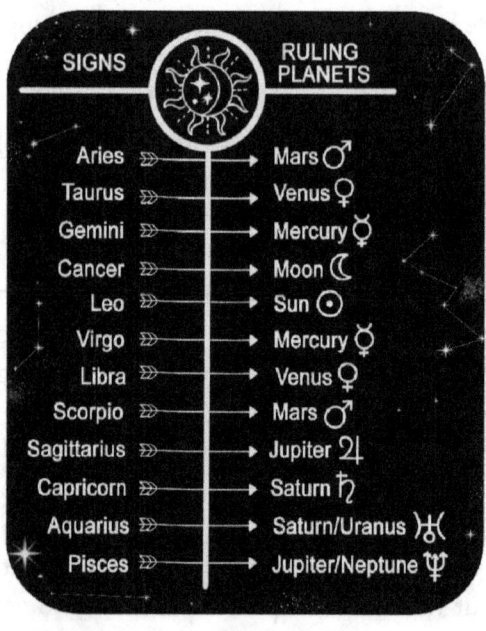

Figure 9 - Signs and Planetary Rulerships

WHO RULES THE ROOST?

Not only are signs connected to their ruling planets, but they are at home in a particular house as well. This is called the ruling house. For example, Aries resides in the first house, the starting position for the first sign on the wheel. Mars is its ruling planet. We can say Mars rules the 1st house of Aries. Or Aries rules the first house. The first house has to do with the "head" of the chart, and Aries' corresponding body part is the head. First house material is also the personality, physical body and how we present to the world. For Aries the Ram, that would be butting headfirst into a situation with the force of the planet Mars.

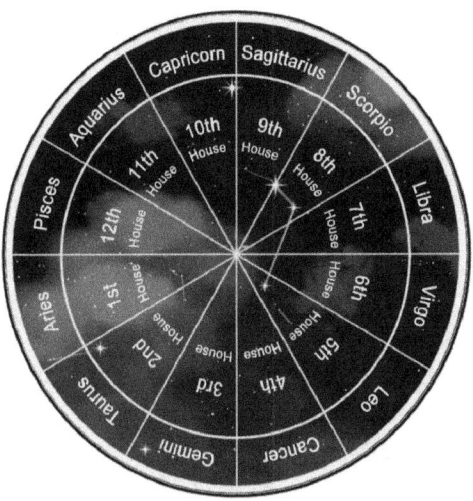

Figure 10 - Signs and the Houses

CHAPTER 5
Astrology Soulmate Placements

When you ask most people familiar with astrology what sign they are compatible with, you will most likely get a very generalized answer about Sun signs. I mean, there are only twelve signs which means looking at compatibility from that alone is almost as limited as reading your horoscope in a newspaper or magazine. Not that this tabloid material lacks validity, but it is far too general of an explanation, considering there are billions of people out there to fit into only twelve definitions.

For example, if you are a Pisces water sign – a general suggestion for a partner would be the other water signs – Scorpio and Cancer, or another Pisces. So, you start your search and soon realize that you really couldn't stand the thought of being with any of these signs for five minutes, much less having a relationship. Perhaps the answer to that is you already have a ton of water sign planets in your personal chart and being with another water sign is like overload. Or maybe the entire rest of your chart is incompatible with Pisces – just because your Suns are in the same element does not mean you would get along. This is only two possibilities of what could be endless scenarios.

The truth is you have a very specialized chart that maps out you and your life in an exceptionally unique way. In fact, the chart is so detailed that you could study it your entire life and continue to gain insight. This book is an attempt to narrow down your choices of compatibilities somewhat, from general to more specific based on certain placements in your individual charts. If you are serious about having a lasting relationship, the next thing you want to look for is a mate that you have enough connections with to make it through the long haul. We meet up with people over and over, lifetime to lifetime. There may be thousands of people you have known more than once, if you think about how many people you encounter in just *one* lifetime. Which means there are thousands (or more) of soulmates out there for you. The key is having enough of the soulmate placements to determine the depth or closeness of previous lives spent together.

In the following chapters I will break down the different aspects of the soulmate quiz which are helpful to understand before taking it.

There are three main areas that are important in determining compatibility between two people:
    1. The Sun Signs
    2. The Sun with the Moon
    3. Venus with Mars

The quiz is broken down into a step-by-step comparison of your charts. Positive connections will get you points. And the points add up to a final compatibility score. The categories are:

Sun Sign Trine Connection
Sun Sign Emotional Connection
Sun Sign Buddy Connection
Sun Sign Mirror Connection
Sun Sign Peer Connection
Sun to Moon Same Sign Friendship Connection
Sun to Moon Opposite Sign Friendship Connection
Venus to Mars Same Sign Sexual Connection
Venus to Mars Opposite Sign Sexual Connection
Sun and Moon in Shared or Opposed Houses
House Sun to House Moon Friendship Connection
Venus and Mars in Shared or Opposed Houses
House Venus to House Mars Sexual Connection
Degree Sun to Moon Friendship Connection
Degree Moon to Sun Friendship Connection
Degree Venus to Mars Sexual Connection
Degree Mars to Venus Sexual Connection
Day Number Compatible Connection

CHAPTER 6
Sun Sign Links

One of the main parts of the Soulmate Quiz is comparing your Sun signs. They represent for the most part your basic natures and makeup. Harmonious Sun signs is one of the strongest indicators of long-term success in relationships, but *you can have a lasting love without Sun connections.* In this chapter we will explore the first five soulmate connections found when comparing your Sun sign with your partner's Sun sign. Obviously, you will share Sun Sign soulmate placements with a lot of people, but you can't have relationships with everyone, nor will you want to. A Sun sign connection alone doesn't guarantee lasting love. But when combined with other soulmate placements (the more the better) your chances increase. To determine if you both share a Sun connection, I have divided this into five easy parts: Sun Sign Trine, Sun Sign Emotional, Sun Sign Buddy, Sun Sign Mirror, and Sun Sign Peer.

Sun Sign Trine Bond

As stated earlier you have a harmonious connection with those who share your own element. Example: If you are a Taurus, you are naturally compatible in a general sense with other earth signs - Taurus, Virgo and Capricorn. The Sun Sign Trine Bond gains two points in the soulmate compatibility quiz because these signs are all a harmonious 120 degrees from each other. A Sun trine Sun aspect means it is easy to understand where the other person is coming from, as their way of expressing is similar to your own. Water signs all operate from an emotional and intuitive perspective, fire signs from a creative adventurous, air signs from an intellectual thought process and earth signs from a practical rational.

Here are the elements again with their associated signs:

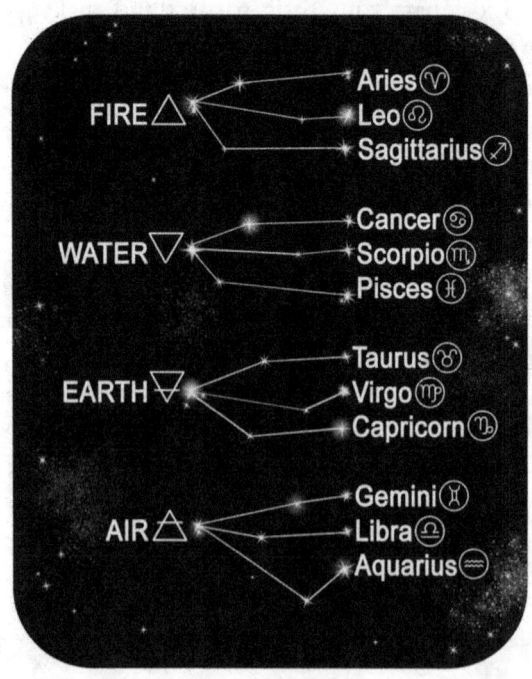

Sun Sign Emotional Bond

In addition to the trine connection, there are certain elements that go together naturally because they have *an emotional understanding*. As a rule, and for the purpose of tallying soulmate "points", the following element combinations are compatible for the long haul because they share the Sun Sign Emotional Bond connection. They are:

- **Earth signs with Air signs**
- **Water signs with Fire signs**

Earth signs have a dry practical approach to emotions, and air signs tend to keep emotional displays in the realm of logic. These two expressions are similar and can bring a sense of commonality that makes you think this person feels and reacts the same to the world as you. It can also show the type of emotional reciprocation both parties would desire from a companion. Water signs have sensitive feelings and intuit their way through life and fire signs outwardly combust with a creative instinctual expression to stimuli. Both react in a more dramatic way when expressing emotion, embracing feelings and letting them flow, giving a basic understanding between these elements.

An example of how elements could react when put in the same situation:

. . .

Let's say a water sign female has four friends – one in each of the elements. She is calling each friend to let them know what happened - her boyfriend has just screwed her over.

The fire sign friend's response to this situation may be, "I can't believe he did that! What a jerk! Are you okay?"

The air sign's response would be something more along the lines of logic such as, "What are you getting so worked up about? He is not worth your time. Forget him and move on."

The earth sign friend's reaction may be silence, followed by some type of practical advice such as, "Do you have enough money to kick him out and live on your own?"

The water sign friend would talk over the various feelings involved, and let her cry, rage or whatever she felt a need to do. And it may be a long conversation, indeed.

Masculine and Feminine Signs

It becomes easy to see how the natural emotional pairing of elements relates to the masculine and feminine qualities of each sign. The masculine element energy is attracted to its feminine counterpart. Masculine is the giving or active essence. Feminine is the passive receptive or receiving essence.

Fire Signs = Masculine

Water Signs = Feminine

Air Signs = Masculine

Earth Signs = Feminine

The masculine fire signs react in an emotional supportive balance to the feminine water signs. The water signs represent compassionate emotional energy to the fire signs who give an active emotional response in return. The masculine air signs react in a mental/rational balance to the feminine earth signs. The earth signs offer practical structure and support to the air signs who give validation to their world.

Sun Sign Buddy Bond

I mentioned earlier that the signs stay in order around the wheel. Your Sun Sign Buddy will come either before or after you in that lineup and will be in a compatible element to yours. Look at the wheel to see which signs sit right next to you.

Reminder - the emotional element compatibilities are:
   Earth signs with Air signs
   Water signs with Fire signs

Find the two signs you are sandwiched between and write down their elements. Only one of those will be in the element that is emotionally compatible with you.

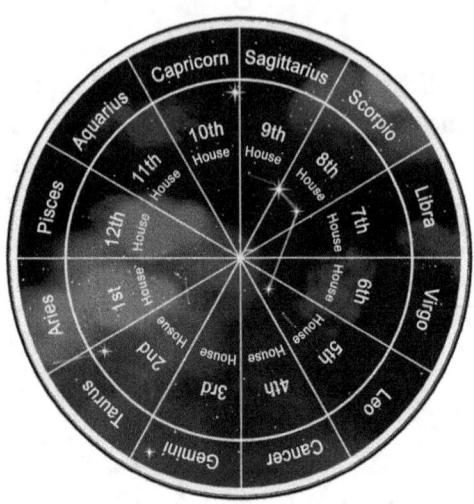

If you are a water sign, your buddy will be the fire sign next to you and vice versa. If you are air your buddy will be the earth sign beside you and vice versa.

Example: Aquarius is an air sign. The emotional element to air is earth. The two signs on either side of Aquarius are Capricorn - earth and Pisces - water. Capricorn is their Sun Sign Buddy.

What can sometimes wreck an otherwise excellent pairing of the Sun Sign Buddy Bond is when the preceding sign gets the feeling that the sign ahead of them is out of reach. This is a common theme. One is behind, the other in front. The one in the lead position seems to be forever unreachable to the other. The partner behind can instinctually feel they must pursue them (either through an intense emotional push or literal active pursuing) which can cause the one in the subsequent position to run, not desiring to be chased. If this dynamic becomes a problem, it is a good idea to slow down and assess each other's needs. If you address the partner doing the pursuing and supply their needs, they may not feel the need to constantly chase you. And if you are smothering or hounding the other, realize they may not like this feeling, so back off and give space. As this placement can be highly compatible for long term, it is wise to take this time to reassess. Where can you recognize and give more to supply the other's needs? (Again, we are talking about healthy individuals capable of having a relationship.)

> Taurus and Gemini are buddies.
> Cancer and Leo are buddies.
> Virgo and Libra are buddies.
> Scorpio and Sagittarius are buddies.
> Capricorn and Aquarius are buddies.
> Pisces and Aries are buddies.

Sun Sign Mirror Bond

Every sign has its opposite, sitting directly across the zodiac wheel. Your opposite sign will not be in a trine or emotional element, but they can be a soulmate connection called the Sun Sign Mirror Bond.

Your opposite or opposing sign can reflect to you, qualities you may be denying in yourself. And although different, they remind you of you. Just like looking in a mirror. These are two individuals who come from opposite ends of the spectrum in opinions but arrive at similar conclusions. The partner could represent the other half of you. But coming from opposite perspectives can be difficult for some to handle, yet for others immensely satisfying.

Opposites attract. They balance things out. Mirrored signs may experience conflict but ultimately the goal is to realize the common ground you share and meet in the middle. The more you take on the traits of your opposite, the more balanced you are as an individual and the closer the two of you become.

Looking at the zodiac wheel, note which sign is directly across from yours.

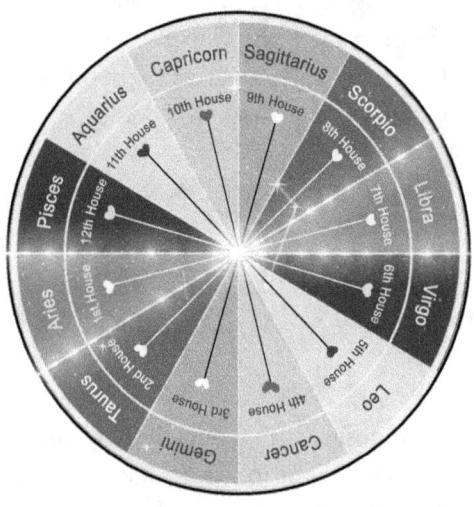

Figure 11 - Opposite Signs on the Wheel

An example of opposite yet harmonious viewpoints: A Scorpio may think that judging others is not a good practice to live by because it is so hurtful to another person (emotional). A Taurus (Scorpio's opposite) may think that judging others - no matter how much they deserve it - only creates division which could cause problems for Taurus' position in life (rational). But both end up with the same conclusion that judging other people is not something they support. Even though it is for different reasons, they can find agreement.

Sun Sign Peer Bond

There is one Sun sign that shares no astrology aspects or angles with yours, therefore you are both on neutral ground. This is called your *parallel* sign, meaning both of your life paths run side by side with each other and do not cross. I call this the Sun Sign Peer bond.

There are no aspects to help or hinder this connection. In terms of karma or past lives, there is a clean slate or the two did not sign up to work through specific karma in this particular lifetime. And even after these two signs get together and experience possible conflicts or problems, it is as if the slate continues to wipe itself clean. The pair can always start anew, if they so choose. I have noticed that two people with this connection seem to share certain things in common, with equal amounts of differences. When two signs are parallel, they lie side by side either going in the same direction from the same point of reference or going in opposite directions. Because of this, both parties need to have common goals, values and belief systems to ensure they travel together in the same direction. I often see a level of spiritual maturity and understanding needed to make this work for the long term. A Peer connection can be a lasting union if the life directions are in harmony with each other. An example would be both parties belonging to the same religion with a shared belief system and following "relationship rules" based on the expectations of that religion. Or having similar beliefs of how their children should be raised.

Parallel or Peer Signs:

Aries and Virgo

Taurus and Sagittarius

Gemini and Scorpio

Cancer and Aquarius

Leo and Capricorn

Libra and Pisces

CHAPTER 7
Best Friends Forever

Friendships last a lifetime and being friends in an intimate relationship gives it value and longevity. We all know beauty fades, so a powerful feeling of kinship can be a solidifier. In an astrology chart, there are ties between the Sun and Moon that signify shared past lives (soulmate) and specifically feelings of friendship. When these planets are connected, it can give you a sense of "being at home" with a person. Even someone you have never met. It is still possible to develop a friendship with a partner though, even if you don't have these shared Sun and Moon placements.

The Sun is masculine and represents the area of your chart where you shine. It is often your dominant nature and the leading influence in your chart. The Moon is feminine and represents what you need to feel safe – the emotional qualities you require to feel loved and how you express emotion. The interactions between the pathways of the Sun and Moon in the heavens is called North and South Nodes. These have a lot to do with your purpose and life path. The Sun and Moon interact together and could have a major impact on whether the two people can get along. The moon sign represents needs on many levels. If the partner's Sun (overall character) is not in harmony with these moon needs, you could feel a sense of not being understood, or a feeling of distance, aloneness, or separation from that person. The same goes for the Sun. If the partner's moon sign and needs is not relating well with your Sun nature, you may be at a loss as far as understanding them or finding basic common ground.

In the quiz, you will explore the three main ways the Sun and Moon can interact between two astrology charts for a friendship link:

1. Occupying the same or opposite sign
2. Houses and rulership connections
3. Sharing the same degree

SAME SIGN FRIENDSHIP BOND

When looking for soulmate past life placements, these heavenly bodies being in the *same* sign are an indicator of a friendship *soulmate* connection. To find the Same Sign Friendship Bond you will first compare your Sun with your partner's Moon to see if they are in the same sign, and then your Moon with your partner's Sun.

For example:
    Your Sun sign – Aries
    Partner's Sun sign - Virgo
    Your Moon sign – Virgo
    Partner's Moon sign – Libra

. . .

Here we have one friendship same sign connection, because your Virgo Moon is in the same sign as your partner's Virgo Sun. Your Aries Sun and your Partner's Libra Moon are not in the same sign, so no same sign connection.

OPPOSITE SIGN FRIENDSHIP BOND

The second friendship placement is having the Sun and Moon in opposite signs. Finding the Opposite Sign Friendship Bond is simply comparing the Sun to the Moon again.

Using the previous example, you both share one Opposite Sign connection because Your Sun in Aries is in the opposite sign of your partner's Moon in Libra.

Your Sun sign – Aries Partner's Sun sign - Virgo
    Your Moon sign – Virgo Partner's Moon sign – Libra

SHARING EACH OTHER'S HOUSE BOND

In earlier chapters we explored finding the planets in your zodiac wheel and their sign and house placement. When searching for more friendship soulmate connections we can look to the houses that the Sun and Moon occupy, and the same or opposite signs connected to the rulership houses. These will be explained in more detail in the quiz.

One example would be having Moon in Aries. You would look to see if your partner had the Sun in the 1st house of Aries. It would also involve looking for same and opposite house sign rulerships.

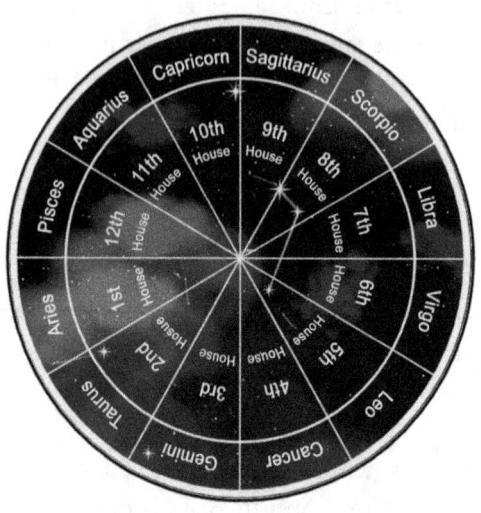

DEGREES OF SEPARATION OR FRIENDSHIP

Another way to check for a friendship sun/moon connection is using degrees. Each of the twelve houses on the zodiac wheel contain thirty degrees and make up a complete circle totaling 360°. When a planet falls into a house, it may be at the beginning of the house, in the middle or near the end. The degrees will indicate this. If your Moon lands in the first house and is halfway through, it may be around lets say the 15° mark. If it is near the end of the first house and close to entering the second house, it may be somewhere near 29°. Once the Moon has exited a house and enters the next it starts at zero degrees again. To find the degree of your Sun and Moon, you will first find the symbol for each planet on your chart. Next to the symbol will be numbers written as something like this: 10°32'. Interpreted, this means the planet is ten degrees and the thirty-two refers to how close it is to getting to eleven degrees. Having the Sun and Moon in the same degree is a soulmate placement. If you feel very bonded to a particular person and there were no sign or house connections between the Sun and Moon, the degree bond could explain your strong feelings of kinship.

In the next chapter we will look at sexual soulmate connections with Venus and Mars.

CHAPTER 8
Hot and Steamy Links

Obviously for any romantic relationship to last you will hopefully have a spark of attraction to the other person. Although this is not always necessary to every relationship, as people can be very different in their wants and needs. To find sexual chemistry in an astrology chart you will be comparing Venus and Mars the exact same way as the Sun and Moon.

Even though Venus and Mars are involved in the sexual aspect of partnerships they can also represent having similar ties of love in common with friends or family. Venus is what you love, how you love, what you want, wish for and how you want to be loved. Mars is how you will get it, how you go after love, what gets you excited, what motivates you, what you are striving to acquire.

Mars and Venus together can represent love, passion and the motivation to express desire. With a lover, these two planets steam things up, whether it is the windows of the car or the tension of attraction that slowly builds on itself. Having these two planets in complementary signs, houses or degrees is going to show a sexual link that gives the relationship the potential to last, the same way the Sun and Moon show natural friendship placements. All four of these planets show past life feelings/desires that are recurring in this life.

Venus is the planet of love and beauty. It strives to find the value in life. What has value? Loyalty, friendship, money or material things? Love? Venus seeks to be loved. The sign you have it in shows how you want to be loved and what you find attractive. Venus from a relationship perspective then, is how you value, view and identify love in someone else.

It is qualities you look for in a partner. Do you want your partner to work hard for the relationship (Venus in Virgo), or do you want someone to stimulate your mind (Venus in Gemini)? Venus is the feminine aspect. In a man's chart, Venus often represents the type of woman he is looking for.

Mars is the planet of energy, drive and passion. What motivates you? What stirs your blood? Where do you want to go? The sign of Mars shows how you express that drive and how you will go after a partner once interested. Do you wait for the person to come to you (Mars in Leo)? Or do you make a beeline to rescue them from the jaws of misfortune (Mars in Aries)? Mars represents the masculine nature. In a woman's chart, Mars can represent the type of man she is looking for.

The feminine and masculine energies of the signs can also affect how a planet expresses itself. For example, an expression of Mars in Taurus (a feminine sign) would be doing things in a slower and more methodical manner. Making sure that everything was safe first, before pursuing a preferably tried-and-true path. With the feminine quality of being receptive, Mars in Taurus might possibly wait for the other person to take the initiative. Mars in Sagittarius (a masculine sign) would think in terms of doing things in a rushed or carefree way. With an attitude of give me space and freedom. Their motto is, "I am outta' here". The masculine Mars in Sagittarius may prefer to be the initiator. Let's compare these two Mars to romantic relationships.

Mars in Taurus may wait for the other to show interest first or wait for the other to introduce themselves before making a move. Followed by a lengthy courting to get to know the other person, and therefore making sure they are a safe bet for the long term. Mars in Sagittarius, however, is the male initiator and would waste no time asking for a first date, followed by playing hard-to-get early into the dating phase - or something similar such as a pulling disappearing act. This is usually to observe a reaction (i.e., how much space/freedom is this person going to give me and be okay with, before I dive in headfirst?) If it is a go, then Mars in Sag suddenly appears at your door with a joke, a grin and your next trip already planned. You leave tonight.

SEXUAL SAME SIGN BOND

Comparing like you did with the Sun and Moon, you will look for a same sign connection between Venus and Mars.

> Your Venus: Gemini/Your Partner's Venus: Aries
> Your Mars: Aries/Your Partner's Mars: Sagittarius

Here we have a sexual connection between your Mars in Aries in the same sign as your partner's Venus in Aries.

SEXUAL OPPOSITE SIGN BOND

Again, you will compare the same as the Sun and Moon looking for an opposite sign attraction. Using the above example:

> Your Venus: Gemini/Your Partner's Venus: Aries
> Your Mars: Aries/Your Partner's Mars: Sagittarius

Your Venus is in Gemini which is the opposite sign to your partner's Mars in Sagittarius, which is a sexual soulmate connection.

LET'S GO TO MY HOUSE BOND

The analysis of sexual attraction follows along the same lines as comparing Sun and Moon for friendship placements in houses. Venus and Mars will connect with their same or opposite rulership houses.

DEGREES OF HEAT BOND

This is the same process as with the Sun and Moon. Having Venus and Mars in the same degree is a soulmate sexual placement. If you have no sign or house connections, the degree bond can explain the attraction you have to a particular person.

TWIN FLAME CONNECTIONS?

There is a lot being bandied about in the new-age movement about "twin flames". Many questions are raised, such as whether they exist, have even incarnated at the same time, or whether you have mistaken a soulmate for a Twin Flame. I do think there is something called a Twin Flame, but I hold the unpopular opinion that these people may be a kind of decoy.

Twin Flames are said to be the other half of your soul, and both parties need to come together to carry out a specific spiritual purpose or mission, that neither can do alone. This to me sounds like a mind-programming agenda, because often the people who think they have met their twin flames are miserable. There always seems to be something separating the two and causing pain – such as both parties being married to someone else or the twin flame being emotionally or spiritually unevolved, unavailable and/or abusive. Very rarely do you hear about a happy couple of Twin Flames – and those parties often are often seen pedaling advice on how to meet your twin, while charging money for their "secrets" with zero guarantees.

I think what is often mistaken for a Twin Flame is actually a person who represents either a negative or positive karmic experience. This to me is a soulmate. But I do think there are other connections outside of soulmates, which could be termed Twin Flames, Twin Selves and Twin Souls. I find that so-called Twin Flames tend to do what the name describes – "burn" up your life. Those who watch my truther videos know that I believe we are in many simulated virtuals inside of virtuals – the world being a matrix. I do believe the Twin Flame teaching to be a possible distraction to keep us from doing the work we came here to do for the world. However, I am not making a blanket or definitive statement here, just researching this possibility. Twin Selves are a replacement for the Twin Flame and could also show no astrology soulmate placements but could have the same affect. The so-called Twin Flame relationships that people talk about are often describing some of the most difficult relationships out there to maintain, because there is a lack of soulmate connections to give the pairing strength for the long term. A lasting relationship would require both parties to be in a similar place in their journey, otherwise this is a relationship that can burn up your life as you pine away when the other partner's flame for you dies.

However, I will say that the charts I have seen with no soulmate connections - yet the person is so "in love" with the other that they cannot let go - could be due to these possibilities:

- The yawning differences in their astrology charts cause a vacuum-like attraction, yet there is suffering and separation. This is likely due to the variances in the charts which are not gelling together, and this relationship would be best to be avoided. These types of pairings are often hallmarked by obsession and a feeling in one of the partners of not being able to let go of or forget the other. This convinces them it must be a Twin Flame relationship, when what they are really experiencing is the agitation between incompatible planetary placements preventing this union. If they continue to interact, causing more suffering, they create new future karma together and would be best to avoid each other and move on with their lives.
- (Twin Soul) Two people find themselves in a happy relationship, yet they have no planetary soulmate connections. This may be a situation where both individuals have *resolved all karma* and can just enjoy each other's company in this life. This connection may actually be the closest to what a Twin Flame relationship is purported to be. I call this a Twin Soul relationship.
- Another reason two people can feel an unusually strong attraction to each other despite little to no planetary soulmate connections, could be that their souls did not choose to be together in this lifetime.

They suffer because they try to force the union. A lack of astrology soulmate connections doesn't mean they have never had past lives together or have other harmonious planetary aspects. It could just mean they did not come into this particular life to live out karma with each other. The soulmate connections being explored in this book are the ones that reveal karma – for good or bad – that we came in to rectify or allow to unfold and enjoy in this lifetime. The planets let us know this.

Some other things to consider:

If you are having trouble coming together with the person you love and experiencing many obstacles to living a fulfilling relationship, *and* there are soulmate connections in your charts, this could very well be a *negative karmic soulmate* connection that you would be best to avoid. You mistakenly believed they were a Twin Flame, when in fact they were a negative "payment" soulmate. Or the person did not do the work on themselves that was needed prior to your "meet cute" and it becomes anything but cute. This leads to "impossible" situations such as already being married, or having children from that marriage that determine whether they decide to stay or go. Religious affiliations that make them incompatible with your beliefs, a history of substance abuse, crimes, ruined credit, a lack of spiritual awareness or effort and many other obstacles that create immediate problems and demonstrate clearly to you that they are not ready. Their soul did not meet you at the original agreed upon point in your lives, but got sidetracked, distracted or made different or bad decisions along the way.

. . .

Another situation that gets mistaken for a Twin Flame relationship (with no soulmate connections) is having both moons conjunct or in the same sign or house. It can be a very strong kinship but not necessarily a relationship with the strength to last.

CHAPTER 9

The Quiz

To make finding soulmate placements easier, I have created a test. It will tally points for each soulmate connection. A higher score can increase the potential of a long-term relationship. You will need your natal charts to follow along. (For more detailed information on the quiz please see Chapters 6 – 8.)

Note: If you do not have your birth time(s) you will not be able to calculate all the connections but can still take the quiz. If you are interested in finding your own or someone else's likely time of birth, you can contact a professional astrologer that specializes in "rectification" charts. Rectifying the birth time is a bit of an involved process, as the astrologer will have to track certain events in your life to determine your likely birth time.

THE SOULMATE CONNECTION QUIZ

When answering the questions, give each connection that you and your partner share one point, unless otherwise noted. You may want to grab a notepad or have somewhere to keep score.

To complete the first section, fill in both of your signs and elements below for a handy reference.

	YOUR'S	PARTNER'S
Sun Sign		
Element		
Moon Sign		
Venus Sign		
Mars Sign		

Figure 12 - Fill in your placements

The first section will cover the *Sun Sign* connections in your charts as Sun Sign rapport is a big factor in having a harmonious relationship. Let's begin!

1. Sun Sign Trine Connection:

Are your Sun Signs in the same element? (Example: Your Sun sign is an air sign and your partner's Sun is also in an air sign, such as Libra and Gemini.)

Connection? _____ (2 Points)

2. Sun Sign Emotional Connection:

Are your Sun signs in compatible elements? (The compatible elements are Earth with Air and Fire with water. An example would be your Sun sign is Virgo-earth and your partner's is in Aquarius-air.) If you answer "yes", check below to see if you also have the Buddy Connection.

Connection? _____ (2 Points)

3. Sun Sign Buddy Connection:

Do your Suns sit right next to each other in compatible elements? (Your Buddy would be either the sign right before or after yours that is in a compatible element – fire with water or earth with air. Taurus is an earth sign and therefore compatible with air. Taurus is sandwiched between Aries-fire and Gemini-air. Since earth and air are compatible, Gemini would be Taurus' Buddy Connection.)

Connection? _____ (1 extra point – Note: If you have this placement, you would have already have #2 The Emotional Connection.)

4. Sun Sign Mirror Connection:

Are your Suns in opposite signs? (Your opposite sign is six signs away from yours. Example: Aries is opposite Libra.)

Connection? _____

5. Sun Sign Peer Connection

Are your Sun signs parallel to each other (see Chapter 6 Parallel signs)?

Connection? _____

. . .

Now you will examine connections between the Sun (basic nature) with the Moon (feelings and needs), and Venus (what you love) with Mars (your drive and passion).

6. Sun to Moon Same Sign Friendship Connection:

Is your Sun in the *same* sign as your partner's Moon? (Example: Your Sun is in Leo and your partner's Moon is in Leo.)
Connection? ____

7. Moon to Sun Same Sign Friendship Connection:
Is your Moon in the *same* sign as your partner's Sun? (Example: Your Moon is in Sagittarius and your partner's Sun is in Sagittarius.)
Connection? ____

8. Sun to Moon Opposite Sign Friendship Connection:
Is your Sun in the *opposite* sign as your partner's Moon? (Example: Your Sun is in Cancer and your partner's Moon is in Capricorn. Cancer is opposite or six signs away from Capricorn.)
Connection? ____

9. Moon to Sun Opposite Sign Friendship Connection:
Is your Moon in the *opposite* sign as your partner's Sun? (Example: Your Moon is in Scorpio and your partner's Sun is in Taurus. Scorpio's opposite sign is Taurus.)
Connection? ____

10. Venus to Mars Same Sign Sexual Connection:
    Is your Venus in the *same* sign as your partner's Mars? (Do the same here as you did for the Sun and Moon.)
    Connection? ____

11. Mars to Venus Same Sign Sexual Connection:
    Is your Mars in the *same* sign as your partner's Venus?
    Connection? ____

12. Venus to Mars Opposite Sign Sexual Connection:
    Is your Venus in the *opposite* sign to your partner's Mars?
    Connection? _____

13. Mars to Venus Opposite Sign Sexual Connection:
    Is your Mars in the *opposite* sign to your partner's Venus?
    Connection? _____

For the next section fill in the following information for reference:

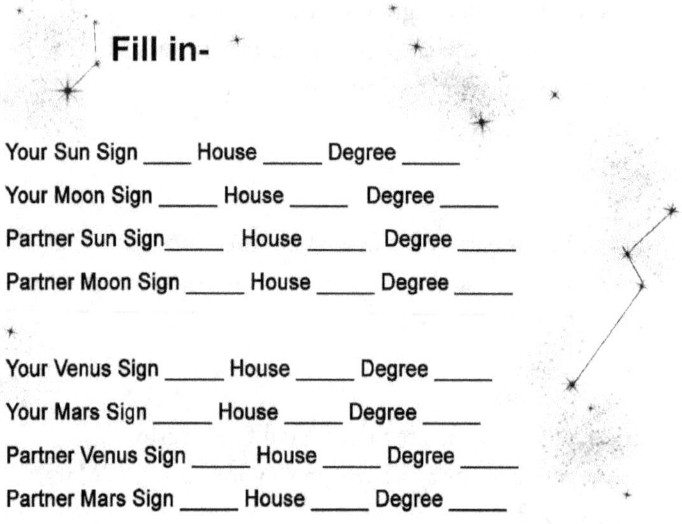

Fill in-

Your Sun Sign _____ House _____ Degree _____
Your Moon Sign _____ House _____ Degree _____
Partner Sun Sign _____ House _____ Degree _____
Partner Moon Sign _____ House _____ Degree _____

Your Venus Sign _____ House _____ Degree _____
Your Mars Sign _____ House _____ Degree _____
Partner Venus Sign _____ House _____ Degree _____
Partner Mars Sign _____ House _____ Degree _____

Figure 13 - Fill in your placements 2

You will also need to reference this chart of opposite Signs and Corresponding Houses

SIGNS OF A SOULMATE

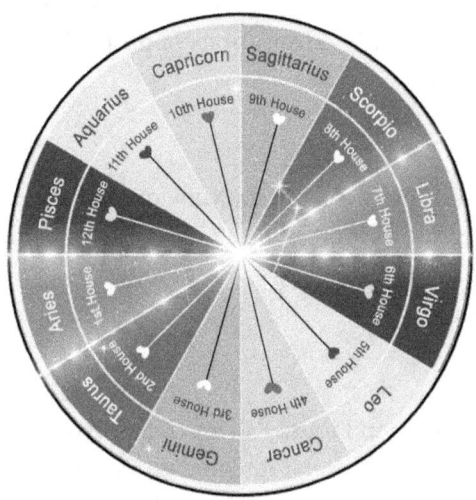

To find the *degrees* of the planets, locate the small number next to your Sun, Moon, Venus and Mars. Let's say your Sun is a little past 20 degrees into a sign, then it may be written something like this: 20°3'. The second number "3" measures how close the Sun is to changing to the next degree of "21".

If you do not have an accurate birth time, you will skip Questions 14 – 19. A time of birth lets you know which houses your planets are in – meaning you *could* have soulmate connections in the houses but would not have the information to know this. So, realize that you could have more soulmate points than what your actual results show, but the test can still give you a fairly accurate read on long term rapport and compatibility, unless you *only* have these placements.

14. Sun and Moon in Shared or Opposed Houses?
    Is your Sun and their Moon in the same or opposite house?

(Example: You have Sun in the 7th House and your partner has their Moon in the 7th House or its opposite – the 1st House.)
Connection? ____

Is their Sun and your Moon in the same or opposite house?
(Example: Your Moon is in the 8th House and their Sun is in the 8th House or its opposite – the 2nd House)
Connection? ____

15. Your Sun to Moon House Ruler Friendship Connection:
Is your partner's Moon in the house that your Sun sign rules? (Reference your astrology charts to see if their Moon is the house of your Sun Sign. For example: If you are a Sun Sign Pisces, you would look to see if your partner has their Moon in the twelfth house – the ruling house of Pisces.)
Connection? ____
Is your Moon in the house that your partner's Sun sign rules?
Connection? ____
Is your partner's Sun in the house that your Moon sign rules? (Reference your astrology charts to see if their Sun is the house of your Moon Sign. For example: If your Moon is in Aries, you would look to see if your partner has their Sun in the first house – the ruling house of Aries.)
Connection? ____
Is your Sun in the house that your partner's Moon sign rules?
Connection? ____

16. Your Sun to Moon Opposite House Ruler Friendship Connection:
Is your partner's Moon in the opposite house that your Sun sign rules? (Reference your astrology charts to see if their Moon is in the opposite house of your Sun Sign. For example: If you are a

Sun Sign Pisces, you would look to see if your partner has their Moon in the sixth house – the house of Virgo – the opposite house of Pisces.)

Connection? ____

Is your Moon in the opposite house that your partner's Sun sign rules?

Connection? ____

Is your partner's Sun in the opposite house that your Moon sign rules? (Reference your astrology charts to see if their Sun is in the opposite house of your Moon Sign. For example: If you are a Moon in Aries, you would look to see if your partner has their Sun in the seventh house – the house of Libra – the opposite house of Aries.)

Connection? ____

Is your Sun in the opposite house that your partner's Moon sign rules?

Connection? ____

17. Venus and Mars in Shared or Opposed Houses?

Is your Venus and their Mars in the same or opposite house?

(Example: You have Venus in the 11th House and your partner has their Mars in the 11th House or its opposite – the 5th House.)

Connection? ____

Is their Venus and your Mars in the same or opposite house?

(Example: Their Venus is in the 7th House and you have your Mars is in the 7th House or its opposite – the 1st House)

Connection? ____

18. Venus to House Mars House Ruler Sexual Connection:

Is your partner's Mars in the house that your Venus sign rules?

(Example: Your Venus sign is Pisces. You would look to see if your partner has their Mars in the 12th house – the house Pisces rules.)

Connection? _____

Is your Mars in the house that your partner's Venus sign rules?

Connection? _____

Is your partner's Venus in the house that your Mars sign rules?

Connection? _____

Is your Venus in the house that your partner's Mars sign rules?

Connection? _____

19. Venus to Mars Opposite House Ruler Sexual Connection:

Is your partner's Mars in the opposite rulership house to your Venus sign?

(Example: Your Venus sign is Gemini. You would look to see if your partner has their Mars in the opposite house which would be the 9th house of Sagittarius - Gemini's opposite house.)

Connection? _____

Is your Mars in the opposite rulership house to your partner's Venus sign?

Connection? _____

Is your partner's Venus in the opposite rulership house to your Mars sign?

Connection? _____

Is your Venus in the opposite rulership house to your partner's Mars sign?

Connection? _____

20. Degree Sun to Moon Friendship Connection:

Is your Sun in the same degree as your partner's Moon?

SIGNS OF A SOULMATE

(To find the degrees, reference your astrology charts and locate the small number next to your Sun and Moon.)
Connection? ____

21. Degree Moon to Sun Friendship Connection:
Is your Moon in the same degree as your partner's Sun?
Connection? ____

22. Degree Venus to Mars Sexual Connection:
Is your Venus in the same degree as your partner's Mars?
(To find the degrees, reference your astrology charts and locate the small number next to your Venus and Mars.)
Connection? ____

23. Degree Mars to Venus Sexual Connection:
Is your Mars in the same degree as your partner's Venus?
Connection? ____

Bonus Point: The Day Number Connection:
Do you have compatible Day Numbers? (These numbers *relate to the planets* and can add another level of long-term compatibility if you are missing the basic Sun Sign connections or do not have a lot of soulmate connections. To calculate, reduce the day you were born to a single number. (If you are born on the 21st of May – 2 + 1 = 3. If you are born on the 17th of the month – 1 + 7 = 8.) When you get both of your single day of birth numbers, compare them to see if they are compatible.

The compatible numbers are as follows:
Each number with their own number - 1 with 1, 2 with 2, 3 with 3, 4 with 4, 5 with 5, 6 with 6, 7 with 7, 8 with 8, 9 with 9.

1, 2, 4 and 7 are also compatible (although a 4 can make life more difficult for a 1).

3, 6 and 9 are compatible

4 is compatible with 8.

Connection? ____

See my book "5 Numbers of Destiny" for more information on numbers.

Now add up all your points from the quiz and read your results in the "scores" that follow.

Scores:

A soulmate refers to past life connections. Realize that not all soulmate connections with another person are happy. Some partners can be "payment karma" soulmates. Meaning you have come together to play out an unhappy scenario in this life, and you would be better off avoiding the continual looping of bad experiences that the two of you continue to share lifetime to lifetime. (Be sure you are considering a person who is sincerely intending to enter a supportive respectful relationship with you, and is not bringing red flags, abusive behaviors and character flaws to the table.) The soulmates you want to focus on and invest time in represent "reward karma" where you can share the benefits of a healthy relationship together based on previous lifetimes of shared happiness.

Burning Love

0 - 1 Connections: This may be a karmic connection that has a purpose to awaken you to yourself, but not necessarily with the potential to last. Often, I see this in charts of people who say they have met their "Twin Flame". This score usually means they can light a fire in each other but one or both usually end up getting burned. Depending on exactly what the agreement was between

these souls, their relationship can possibly go the distance but often devolves fairly quickly. Read below to see if this score is positive or unfortunate for your relationship.

A low score could represent a Twin Flame or Twin Self relationship. The two of you are at a similar place in your soul journey, and you both decided to meet at a certain point in this life because one of you wanted to help the other in some way - whether for your own good or not. With a Twin Flame or Twin Self, there is such a marked difference in the astrology charts that it takes on an "opposites attract" characteristic only with a twist. This is not a natural "opposition" aspect but rather two people who are completely different from each other. There is very little glue in the charts to hold them together through good times and bad. And it is anyone's guess which there will be more of – the good or the bad. To know if you are in a Twin Flame or Twin Self relationship, they are usually identified by obsessive feelings or a pining for the other, an inability to let go and a determination to make the impossible happen when unable to be with the other person (whether they want you or not). After the initial high of meeting the twin, the relationship is often marked by a corresponding crash into emotional agony, depression, guilt, grief and pain. Most likely, the two of you did not come into this life to work out karma together (this may be for another lifetime – or you already have worked through what was needed) but you have chosen to find this person again, regardless. Either party holding on to the other or continuing to interact when it is clear you cannot be together will create new negative karma in this life. By not letting go, you prevent your life from moving forward and get derailed from accomplishing your purpose or meeting a partner who can support you. In essence, holding on is holding you back. Remember, you do not need anyone else to accomplish your spiritual purpose or follow your life path.

. . .

The good news is that a score of 0 – 1 can represent what I call a "Twin Soul". This is a person who is deeply connected to you on a soul level and can forge through this journey of life with you. Together you generate feelings of being "two peas in a pod". This represents a pair of souls who have no karmic connections in the chart and may be part of the same soul. A Twin Soul relationship is marked by feelings of joy, interconnectedness and ease. This may be a term to describe what has been written about a Twin Flame relationship – but keep in mind I am using my own terms here to differentiate. Sometimes a Twin Soul is mistaken for a soulmate, but taking this quiz helps you know the difference.

Read my section on "Twin Flames" in the previous chapter for more on this subject.

Budding Romance
2 – 4 Connections: Even though on the lower end of the scale, it is certainly a soulmate connection. You will need to work on possible differences for long-term harmony. This relationship can be more common to those shared with a friend or someone in your social circle. A Budding Romance connection may not create a tight enough bond for intimate relationships to go the distance, unless you are transparent with each other and have a clear intent to develop the relationship moving forward. This pairing has an energy of "getting to know each other and building something new" in this life but can be lasting if you are both emotionally mature and willing to work at it. You will have to protect the union from outside influences. There may also be a reason you came together that is not romantic – such as business or some other venture that would be more beneficial than romance.

. . .

Shooting Star

5 – 7 Connections: A great score that defines true soulmates. The two of you met and there were stars in your eyes ever since. This partnership has the potential to be long-lasting, although like any relationship you will have to work on occasional difficulties or challenges and embrace your differences to keep the spark alive. But with this many points it is worth the effort to try. An astrology "synastry chart" can show additional harmonious factors – aspects between the planets and placements that increase compatibility and help solidify your bond. However, with a lot of difficult aspects or conflicting placements this could be a shooting star that aims high, burns hot and bright but could just as quickly burn out.

Positive Friction

8 - 10 Connections: This is an amazingly strong and beautiful connection. There is a lot of admiration and appreciation on both sides. Like two magnets drawn together, it was next to impossible that you wouldn't find each other in this lifetime. You feel supported and meet on common ground. The feeling is that you "know" the other person and have been together before. Probably through many lifetimes. There should be minimal conflict, but as every situation is unique this is not a hard fast rule. Issues could come up if each party is not in the place they need to be, to have a functional relationship. In that case, nurture strong communication skills and focus on your similarities, working through any difficult times with understanding and determination. It will be worth it in the long run, because you both can definitely be there for the long haul.

Blissful Union

11 or more Connections: This could be one of those fairy tale relationships that romance books are written about. Your chances of a long-term relationship are greatly enhanced, almost taking on the magical or uncanny and has the feeling of an inseparable merging of souls and minds. There should be more than enough positive energy to get you through to the happily ever after. Keep in mind that both parties need to be at a healthy emotional and mental place no matter how good the harmony and connection. I give this warning, because the pull is so strong between these two that the danger would be to ignore red flags - one partner being emotionally unhealthy, yet you enter the relationship anyway against better judgement. But overall, this should be a solid happy union if both parties are ready and suitable for a healthy commitment.

If you do not have a lot of soulmate connections: It may be worth researching into the Destiny or Life Path number compatibility in Pythagorean Numerology to see if there is additional harmony that can help the relationship. And realize that there are always exceptions to every rule. Nothing in this matrix world is ever 100%. *There is always the anomaly.*

Also keep in mind that there are many factors that can help compatibility such as having your Moon, Venus or Mars in the same sign. They may not guarantee longevity but can create added harmony.

CHAPTER 10
Real Life Soulmates

Let's explore an example of two people, Cindy and Justin, and their respective charts. Figure 1 is Cindy's chart, printed on Astro.com. The second is Justin's chart, printed on Kepler software. I used two different programs to show you how the wheels can look a bit different, depending on what you use. But they will be read in exactly the same way. In Cindy's chart, you will notice that the 9th and 10th houses are not directly at the top of her chart, but slightly over to the left. In Justin's chart, the 10th house is nicely lined up at the top of his wheel. If your chart layout looks different than these, it will not alter the interpretation.

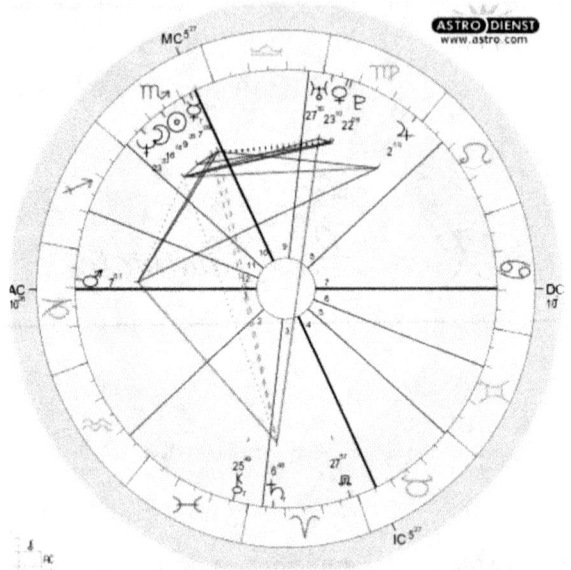

Figure 14 - Cindy's Chart

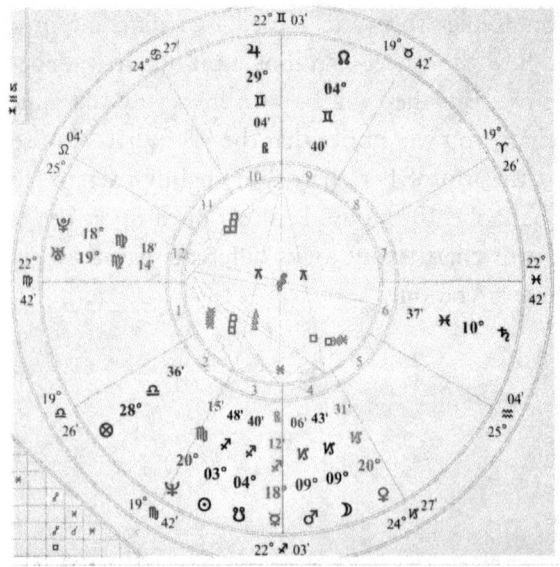

Figure 15 - Justin's Chart

SIGNS OF A SOULMATE

Cindy is wanting to take the Soulmate Quiz to see if Justin is her soulmate. To begin, she will reference both of their charts and identify what signs the Sun, Moon, Venus and Mars are in to gather the information she needs for the quiz.

We can see that Cindy has her Sun and Moon both in Scorpio. Justin has his Sun in Sagittarius and his Moon in Capricorn. Cindy has her Venus in Virgo and Mars in Capricorn. Justin has both Venus and Mars in Capricorn.

I have already entered these into the chart below for easy reference:

	YOUR'S	PARTNER'S
Sun Sign	Scorpio	Sagittarius
Element	Water	Fire
Moon Sign	Scorpio	Capricorn
Venus Sign	Virgo	Capricorn
Mars Sign	Capricorn	Capricorn

Figure 16 - Cindy and Justin's Placements

For the first section of the quiz Cindy will compare both Sun Signs to look for compatibility, answering questions 1-5 followed by questions 6 – 13 comparing the Sun with the Moon and Venus with Mars.

1. Sun Sign Trine Connection:
   Are your Sun Signs in the same element?
   Connection? _____ (2 Points)
   Cindy and Justin's are water and fire - 0 points.

2. Sun Sign Emotional Connection:
   Are your Sun signs in compatible elements? (Check below to see if you also have the Buddy Connection.)
   Connection? _____ (2 Points)
   Cindy and Justin have their Suns in water and fire which is compatible – 2 points.

3. Sun Sign Buddy Connection:
   Do your Suns sit right next to each other in compatible elements?
   Connection? _____ (1 extra point – Note: If you have this placement, you will also have #2 The Emotional Connection.)
   Cindy and Justin have this connection since Scorpio and Sagittarius sit next to each other and are element buddies – 1 point.

4. Sun Sign Mirror Connection:
   Are your Suns in opposite signs?
   Connection? _____
   Cindy and Justin get 0 points.

5. Sun Sign Peer Connection

SIGNS OF A SOULMATE

Are your Sun signs parallel to each other? (See chapter on Parallel signs)
Connection? ____
Cindy and Justin get 0 points.

6. Sun to Moon Same Sign Friendship Connection:
Is your Sun in the *same* sign as your partner's Moon?
Connection? ____
Cindy has Sun in Scorpio which is not the same sign as Justin's Moon in Capricorn – 0 points.

7. Moon to Sun Same Sign Friendship Connection:
Is your Moon in the *same* sign as your partner's Sun?
Connection? ____
Cindy has Moon in Scorpio which is not in the same sign as Justin's Sun in Sagittarius – 0 points.

8. Sun to Moon Opposite Sign Friendship Connection:
Is your Sun in the *opposite* sign as your partner's Moon?
Connection? ____
Cindy's Sun is Scorpio. The opposite of Scorpio is Taurus. Justin's Moon is not in Taurus – 0 points.

9. Moon to Sun Opposite Sign Friendship Connection:
Is your Moon in the *opposite* sign as your partner's Sun?
Connection? ____
Cindy's Moon is in Scorpio. Justin's Sun is in Sagittarius. The opposite of Sagittarius is Gemini – 0 points.

10. Venus to Mars Same Sign Sexual Connection:

Is your Venus in the *same* sign as your partner's Mars? Connection? ____

Cindy's Venus is in Virgo which is not the same sign as Justin's Mars in Capricorn – *0 points.*

11. Mars to Venus Same Sign Sexual Connection:

Is your Mars in the *same* sign as your partner's Venus? Connection? ____

Cindy's Mars is in Capricorn. Justin's Venus is in Capricorn – *1 point.*

12. Venus to Mars Opposite Sign Sexual Connection:

Is your Venus in the *opposite* sign to your partner's Mars? Connection? ____

Cindy's Venus is in Virgo. The opposite of Virgo is Pisces. Justin's Mars is in Capricorn. The opposite of Capricorn is Cancer – *0 points.*

13. Mars to Venus Opposite Sign Sexual Connection:

Is your Mars in the *opposite* sign to your partner's Venus? Connection? ____

Cindy's Mars is in Capricorn. Justin's Venus is in Capricorn. The opposite of Capricorn is Cancer – *0 points.*

For the next section Cindy will fill in more detailed information from their natal charts such as house and degree of each planet to use for questions 14 – 23. I have already entered the information into the reference chart:

Your Sun Sign Scorpio House 10th Degree 9
Your Moon Sign Scorpio House 10th Degree 10
Partner Sun Sign Sagittarius House 3rd Degree 3
Partner Moon Sign Capricorn House 4th Degree 9

Your Venus Sign Virgo House 8th Degree 23
Your Mars Sign Capricorn House 12th Degree 7
Partner Venus Sign Capricorn House 4th Degree 20
Partner Mars Sign Capricorn House 4th Degree 9

Figure 17 - Cindy and Justin's Placements 2

14. Sun and Moon in Shared or Opposed Houses
Is your Sun and their Moon in the same or opposite house? Connection? ____
Cindy's Sun is in the 10th House. Justin's Moon is in the 4th House. The opposite houses would be the 10th or the 4th – 1 Point.
Is their Sun and your Moon in the same or opposite house? Connection? ____
Justin's Sun is in the 3rd House. Cindy's Moon is in the 10th House. The opposite houses would be the 9th or 4th House – 0 points.

15. Your Sun to Moon House Ruler Friendship Connection:
Is your partner's Moon in the house that your Sun sign rules? Connection? ____
Justin's Moon is in the 4th house of Cancer. Cindy's Sun is in Scorpio – 0 points.
Is your Moon in the house that your partner's Sun sign rules? Connection? ____
Cindy's Moon is in the 10th house of Capricorn. Justin's Sun is in Sagittarius – 0 points.
Is your partner's Sun in the house that your Moon sign rules?

Connection? ____

Justin's Sun is in the 3rd house of Gemini. Cindy's Moon is in Scorpio – 0 points.

Is your Sun in the house that your partner's Moon sign rules?
Connection? ____

Cindy's Sun is in the 10th house of Capricorn. Justin's Moon is in Capricorn – 1 point.

16. Your Sun to Moon Opposite House Ruler Friendship Connection:

Is your partner's Moon in the opposite house that your Sun sign rules?
Connection? ____

Justin's Moon is in the 4th house of Cancer. Cindy's Sun sign is Scorpio. The opposite of Scorpio is Taurus – 0 points.

Is your Moon in the opposite house that your partner's Sun sign rules?
Connection? ____

Cindy's Moon is in the 10th house of Capricorn. Justin's Sun sign is Sagittarius. The opposite of Sagittarius is Gemini – 0 points.

Is your partner's Sun in the opposite house that your Moon sign rules?
Connection? ____

Justin's Sun is in the 3rd house of Gemini. Cindy's Moon is in Scorpio. The opposite of Scorpio is Taurus – 0 points.

Is your Sun in the opposite house that your partner's Moon sign rules?
Connection? ____

Cindy's Sun is in the 10th house of Capricorn. Justin's Moon sign is Capricorn. The opposite of Capricorn is Cancer – 0 points.

17. Venus and Mars in Shared or Opposed Houses?

Is your Venus and their Mars in the same or opposite house?

Connection? ____

Cindy's Venus is in the 8th house. Justin's Mars is in the 4th house. The opposite houses would be the 2nd or 10th - 0 points.

Is their Venus and your Mars in the same or opposite house?
Connection? ____

Justin's Venus is in the 4th House. Cindy's Mars is in the 12th House. The opposite houses would be the 10th or 6th - 0 points.

18. Venus to House Mars House Ruler Sexual Connection:

Is your partner's Mars in the house that your Venus sign rules?

Connection? ____

Justin's Mars is in the 4th house of Cancer. Cindy's Venus is in Virgo - 0 points.

Is your Mars in the house that your partner's Venus sign rules?

Connection? ____

Cindy's Mars is in the 12th house of Pisces. Justin's Venus is in Capricorn - 0 points.

Is your partner's Venus in the house that your Mars sign rules?

Connection? ____

Justin's Venus is in the 4th house of Cancer. Cindy's Mars is in Capricorn - 0 points.

Is your Venus in the house that your partner's Mars sign rules?

Connection? ____

Cindy's Venus is in the 8th house of Scorpio. Justin's Mars is in Capricorn - 0 points.

19. Venus to Mars Opposite House Ruler Sexual Connection:

Is your partner's Mars in the opposite rulership house to your Venus sign?

Connection? ____

Justin's Mars is in the 4th house of Cancer. Cindy's Venus is in Virgo. The opposite of Virgo is Pisces – 0 points.

Is your Mars in the opposite rulership house to your partner's Venus sign?

Connection? ____

Cindy's Mars is in the 12th house of Pisces. Justin's Venus is in Capricorn. The opposite of Capricorn is Cancer – 0 points.

Is your partner's Venus in the opposite rulership house to your Mars sign?

Connection? ____

Justin's Venus is in the 4th house of Cancer. Cindy's Mars is in Capricorn. The opposite of Capricorn is Cancer – 1 point.

Is your Venus in the opposite rulership house to your partner's Mars sign?

Connection? ____

Cindy's Venus is in the 8th house of Scorpio. Justin's Mars is in Capricorn. The opposite of Capricorn is Cancer – 0 points.

20. Degree Sun to Moon Friendship Connection:

Is your Sun in the same degree as your partner's Moon?

Connection? ____

Cindy's Sun is 9 degrees and Justin's Moon is 9 degrees – 1 point.

21. Degree Moon to Sun Friendship Connection:

Is your Moon in the same degree as your partner's Sun?

Connection? ____

Cindy's Moon is 10 degrees and Justin's Sun is 3 degrees – 0 points.

22. Degree Venus to Mars Sexual Connection:

SIGNS OF A SOULMATE

Is your Venus in the same degree as your partner's Mars?
Connection? ____

Cindy's Venus is 23 degrees and Justin's Mars is 9 degrees – 0 points.

23. Degree Mars to Venus Sexual Connection:
Is your Mars in the same degree as your partner's Venus?
Connection? ____

Cindy's Mars is 7 degrees and Justin's Venus is 20 degrees – 0 points.

Bonus Points: The Day Number Connection:
Do you have compatible Day Numbers?
Connection? ____

Cindy's Day Number is 2. Justin's Day Number is 26/8. Two and eight are not in a compatible series. 0 points.

Cindy and Justin's totals = 8 Points
Results:
Positive Friction
8 - 10 Connections: This is an amazingly strong and beautiful connection. There is a lot of admiration and appreciation on both sides. Like two magnets drawn together, it was next to impossible that you wouldn't find each other in this lifetime. You feel supported and meet on common ground. The feeling is that you "know" the other person and have been together before. Probably through many lifetimes. There should be minimal conflict, but as every situation is unique this is not a hard fast rule. Issues could come up if each party is not in the place they need to be, to have a functional relationship. In that case, nurture strong communication skills and focus on your similarities, working through any difficult times with understanding and determination. It will be worth it in the long run, because you both can definitely be there for the long haul.

It is worth noting that in real life this relationship did not last, despite having such a high score. One of the individuals has passed on. I have changed the names for privacy and am not revealing locations or other information. I am only relaying the details I was made aware of. Justin's dad died when he was under the age of ten. His mother was an alcoholic and kicked him out of the house at age fourteen. There was no love in his upbringing, and he was on the streets alone as a teen. Even with such overwhelming odds against him, Justin became determined to finish school and make something of himself. He graduated and got a good job. When he met Cindy, the sparks were undeniable, but he had already entered into a toxic marriage with a woman who was diagnosed with a narcissist borderline personality disorder. Cindy became Justin's refuge from the chaos at home. He had led Cindy to believe he was already in the process of getting a divorce when they met – even going to the extent of telling her he had moved out and inviting Cindy to his "new" house (it turned out to be a rental property he owned). And when Cindy realized the many lies she was being told, she wanted out of the situation but the pull to Justin was too strong. Instead of cutting contact, she insisted he get the divorce. Afraid to lose Cindy, Justin briefly considered divorcing his wife until his lawyer informed him he would lose most of his money to the wife in the settlement (even though he could have easily made more as he had an above average income). Justin told Cindy he couldn't go through with a divorce saying, "I guess I love money more than anything else." The wife found emails between the pair, after Cindy had already walked away from the situation, and retaliated in damaging ways taking her anger out on Cindy.

If you look at Justin's chart, he told Cindy the truth (Sun in Sagittarius) about his love of money (Venus and Moon in Capricorn). He has the Mars in the 4th house creating a drive to find roots but also representing anger and control issues at home. Capricorn in the 4th house creates the desire to maintain public image through finances and presenting a solid home life. Moon in Capricorn in the 4th house points to possible abuse and abandonment from both parents. Also, the misguided love of money replacing real love in his Moon in Capricorn placement combined with his Venus in Capricorn. Justin went to a therapist and was eventually diagnosed as a sociopath, so this is a good example of what I said in earlier chapters about some soulmates being "payment" karma. Not all soulmates should be considered for a partnership, no matter how high the score.

CHAPTER 11
Written in the Stars – Famous Couples

Celebrity charts are interesting to compare because many of the details about their relationships have been made public. This gives us information to perhaps back up what is seen in their charts, without invading anyone's privacy. I needed examples of couples that had publicly recorded birth times. Keep in mind that we do not know if these birth times are correct, or whether a couple is happy together. We do not see what goes on behind the closed doors of famous people lives. Sometimes couples choose to stay together even if they aren't getting along. There are many reasons to stay in a relationship. Our personal perceptions of their relationships may not always be reality.

Kurt Russell & Goldie Hawn

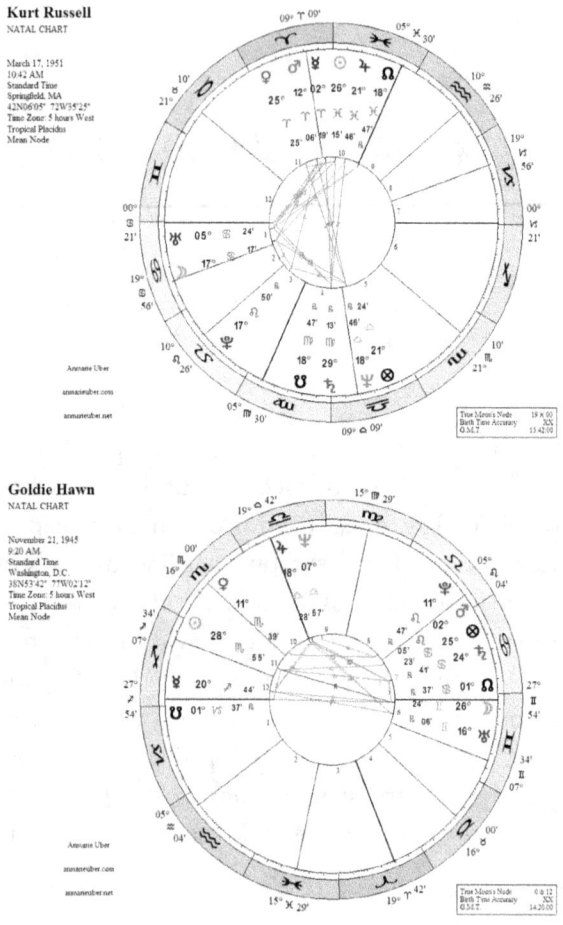

These two actors have been together since 1983. They have several soulmate placements:

Their Suns are Trine

Kurt has Venus in the 11th House of Aquarius which is opposite Goldie's Mars in Leo

Kurt's Sun in Pisces is connected to Goldie's Moon in the House of Virgo

Kurt's Venus is in Aries and Goldie's Mars is in the opposite rulership house of Libra

Kurt's Sun is 26 degrees and Goldie's Moon is 26 degrees

Goldie's Venus is in a late 11 degrees which is very close to Kurt's Mars in early 12 degrees

Score: 7

Results: **Shooting Star**

5 – 7 Connections: A great score that defines true soulmates. The two of you met and there were stars in your eyes ever since. This partnership has the potential to be long-lasting, although like any relationship you will have to work on occasional difficulties or challenges and embrace your differences to keep the spark alive. But with this many points it is worth the effort to try. An astrology "synastry chart" can show additional harmonious factors – aspects between the planets and placements that increase compatibility and help solidify your bond. However, with a lot of difficult aspects or conflicting placements this could be a shooting star that aims high, burns hot and bright but could just as quickly burn out.

Let's see how these results measure up with what these two have said about their relationship and keeping love alive:

Goldie has said publicly that what keeps them together is communication and the freedom of not being married. She has said that if they committed legally on paper the relationship would already be over. On receiving their stars on the Hollywood Walk of Fame, Kurt said:

"Simply put, Goldie, I cherish you. All of the stars in the sky or on the boulevard don't hold a candle to that." [1]

Goldie responded:

"Did we just get married?"

. . .

Pretty accurate statement that reflects their results as two "Shooting Stars".

Anne Heche & Ellen Degeneres

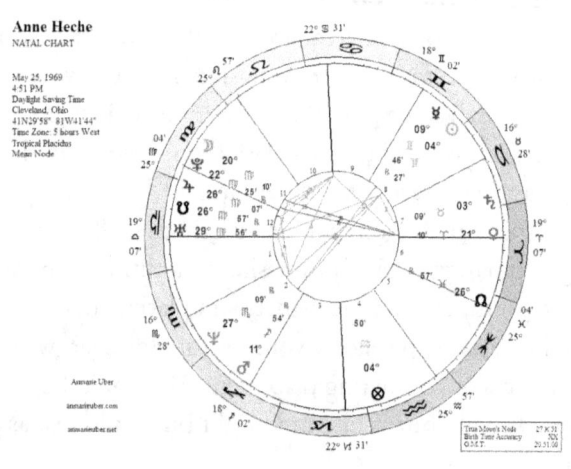

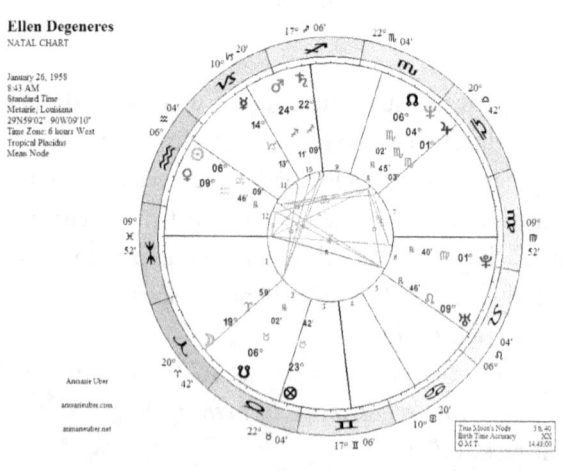

This pair became famous for coming out as an openly gay couple. Their relationship lasted three and a half years followed by a very sudden breakup. Let's take a look at how strong their soulmate connections are.

Score: 4

I noted that their birth numbers are incompatible – 7 and 8 – which causes added conflict.

Results: **Budding Romance**

2 – 4 Connections: Even though on the lower end of the scale, it is certainly a soulmate connection. You will need to work on possible differences for long-term harmony. This relationship can be more common to those shared with a friend or someone in your social circle. A Budding Romance may not create a tight enough bond for intimate relationships to go the distance, unless you are transparent with each other and have a clear intent to develop the relationship moving forward. This pairing has an energy of "getting to know each other and building something new" in this life but can be lasting if you are both emotionally mature and willing to work at it. You will have to protect the union from outside influences. There may also be a reason you came together that is not romantic – such as business or some other venture that would be more beneficial than romance.

At this time, we don't know the full details of what happened, as both have kept silent about their breakup. A quote from Anne reveals their score quite nicely:

"My story is a story that created change in the world, moved the needle for equal rights forward, when I fell in love with Ellen DeGeneres."[2]

This may be a good example of the "Budding Romance" score that hinted at a higher purpose or reason for the two coming together.

Ellen Degeneres & Portia de Rossi

Ellen moved on from the breakup with Anne to be with Portia. They have been together since 2004. Let's look at how their charts match up for better or worse than Ellen and Anne's.

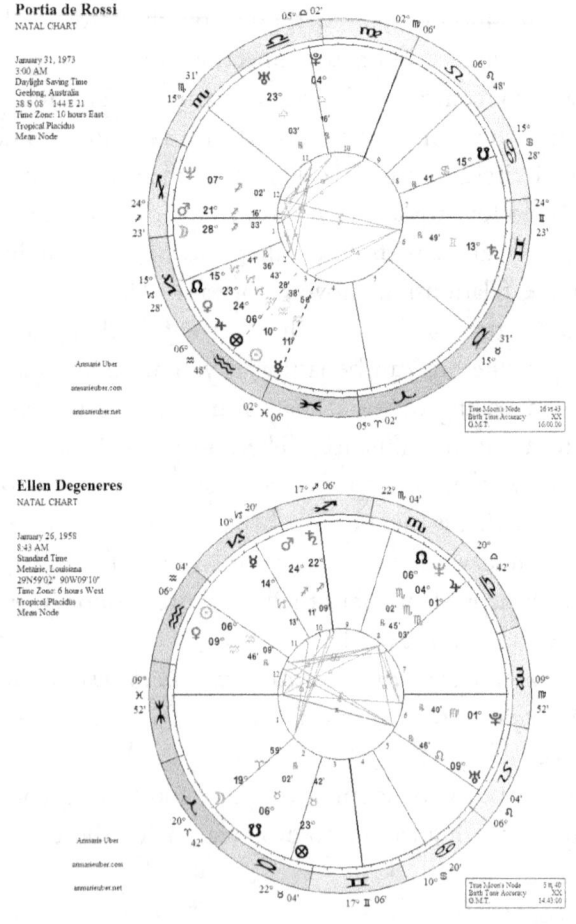

These two have complementary birth numbers - 4 and 8. Their Suns are both Aquarius.

Mars and Venus both close to 24 degrees
Venus and Mars both in the 12th house
Venus in Capricorn and Mars in the house of Capricorn
Score: 5
Results: **Shooting Star**

5 – 7 Connections: A great score that defines true soulmates. The two of you met and there were stars in your eyes ever since. This partnership has the potential to be long-lasting, although like any relationship you will have to work on occasional difficulties or challenges and embrace your differences to keep the spark alive. But with this many points it is worth the effort to try. An astrology "synastry chart" can show additional harmonious factors – aspects between the planets and placements that increase compatibility and help solidify your bond. However, with a lot of difficult aspects or conflicting placements this could be a shooting star that aims high, burns hot and bright but could just as quickly burn out.

As of this writing, the pair is still together. A quote from Portia on her initial feelings about Ellen sums up the feelings with a Shooting Star result – especially with several Venus and Mars connections:

"It was like an arrow shot through my heart. I was weak at the knees; I was overwhelmed with how I felt." [3]

Will Smith & Jada Pinkett Smith
These two actors have been together since 1997. Let's check out their scores.

ANMARIE UBER

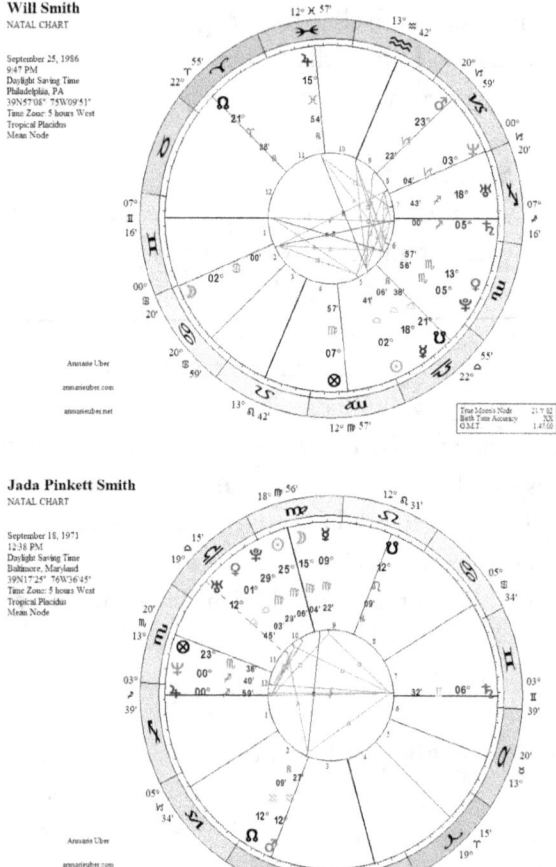

Score: 7

Results: **Shooting Star**

5 – 7 Connections: A great score that defines true soulmates. The two of you met and there were stars in your eyes ever since. This partnership has the potential to be long-lasting, although like any relationship you will have to work on occasional difficulties or challenges and embrace your differences to keep the spark alive. But with this many points it is worth the effort to try. An astrology "synastry chart" can show additional harmonious factors – aspects between the planets and placements that increase

compatibility and help solidify your bond. However, with a lot of difficult aspects or conflicting placements this could be a shooting star that aims high, burns hot and bright but could just as quickly burn out.

Will sums up their success:
"20 Years Ago Today we held hands and walked naively down that aisle. Here's what I've learned since. Love is Like Gardening... I have learned to focus on HELPING you to BLOSSOM into what YOU want to be (into what you were born to be)... Rather than Demanding that you become what my Fragile Ego needs you to be. *If there is a secret I would say is that we never went into working in our relationship. We only ever worked on ourselves individually, and then presented ourselves to one another better than we were previously.*"⁴

Will posted on his Facebook page:
"I have sung happy birthday to you 20 times and I have bought you 19 birthday presents (I was mad that one year). I have watched you blow out 693 candles (737 after tonite). I've told you "I love you" at least 8,285 times. And of the nearly 3.96 Billion women on the planet - there is only 1 that I want to spend the rest of my life with. Happy Birthday, my Love!"
Jada's response was, "You have a 100 percent of my heart and for the rest of my days."

Sarah Michelle Gellar and Freddie Prinze Jr.

This pair has been together since 2002. Let's see their score.

ANMARIE UBER

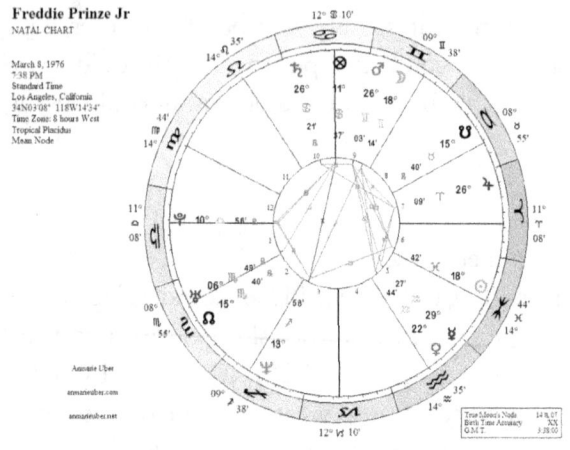

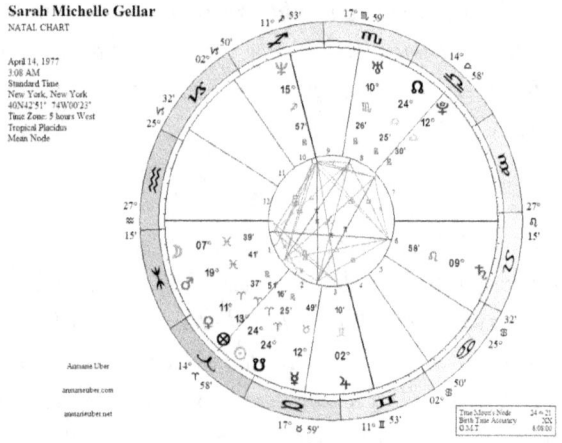

They share:
 Sun Emotional
 Sun Buddies
 Moon and Sun in Pisces
 Sun in the Virgo house and Moon in Pisces

I could count a 6th placement if I look at Pisces overlapping Freddie's 5th house which would connect his Venus to Sarah Michelle's Mars in Pisces.

. . .

Score: 5 (6)
   Results: **Shooting Star**
   5 – 7 Connections: A great score that defines true soulmates. The two of you met and there were stars in your eyes ever since. This partnership has the potential to be long-lasting, although like any relationship you will have to work on occasional difficulties or challenges and embrace your differences to keep the spark alive. But with this many points it is worth the effort to try. An astrology "synastry chart" can show additional harmonious factors – aspects between the planets and placements that increase compatibility and help solidify your bond. However, with a lot of difficult aspects or conflicting placements this could be a shooting star that aims high, burns hot and bright but could just as quickly burn out.

Gellar on their relationship:
   "It's work. You have to work at anything. It's any relationship in your life. You have to nurture it and take time with it." [5]

Pretty good advice for this Shooting Star ranking.

Michael Jackson & Lisa Marie Presley

I was interested to see the connections between these two musicians. This seemed like an odd couple but then I thought about how isolated Michael Jackson was from society, which was similar to the type of life Elvis Presley was forced to live, both being mega-stars. Michael and Lisa Marie's marriage lasted just short of two years.

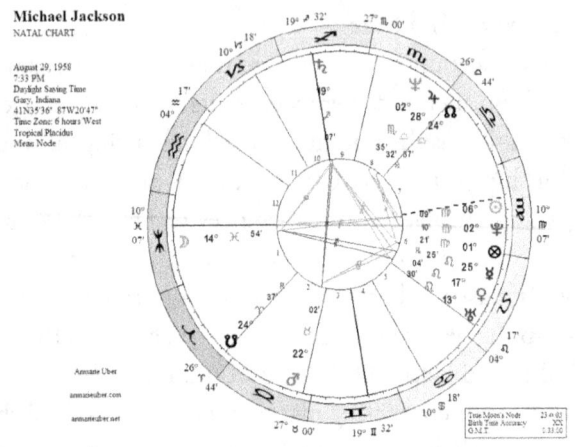

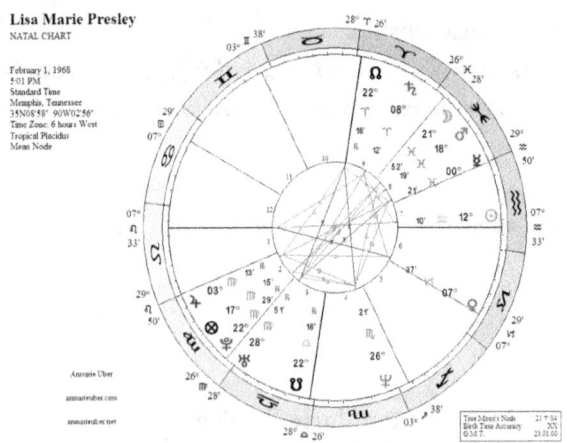

Score: 8

Results: **Positive Friction**

8 - 10 Connections: This is an amazingly strong and beautiful connection. There is a lot of admiration and appreciation on both

sides. Like two magnets drawn together, it was next to impossible that you wouldn't find each other in this lifetime. You feel supported and meet on common ground. The feeling is that you "know" the other person and have been together before. Probably through many lifetimes. There should be minimal conflict, but as every situation is unique this is not a hard fast rule. Issues could come up if each party is not in the place they need to be, to have a functional relationship. In that case, nurture strong communication skills and focus on your similarities, working through any difficult times with understanding and determination. It will be worth it in the long run, because you both can definitely be there for the long haul.

They had several placements, including the Sun and Moon in opposite houses as well as the harmonious birth numbers of 1 and 2.

And wow, what a score! If Michael was going to marry anyone, it would be Lisa Marie. With a Positive Friction score of 8 they are star-crossed lovers with most likely many past lives together.

Lisa Marie left her long-time husband and father of her children to be with Michael. This level of connection is usually too strong to resist. But even with such an exceptional score one or both parties had too many unresolved personal issues preventing them from being in a healthy relationship together. This may be the perfect example of a highly compatible couple who could not make it last due to issues only they can comment on.

While Michael was silent about his feelings, Lisa Marie publicly opened up to the press:

"I absolutely fell in love with him. I loved taking care of him. It was one of the highest points in my life when things were going really well, and he and I were united. It was a very profound time of my life."

. . .

Many sources have quoted Donald Trump as saying the pair were seen "holding hands and talking into the wee hours" when they met. They were also reported to have been getting snuggly in a park where they would "hold hands, kiss and cuddle, stare into each other's eyes and look out at the stars."[6]

Elvis & Priscilla

And speaking of Presleys, I also wanted to look at Priscilla and Elvis.

Elvis had a chart done in Larry Geller's book, "If I can Dream," that shows a different birth time than what comes up for Elvis publicly. That chart makes more sense, with Scorpio and Sagittarius on the rise reflecting Elvis' magnetic presence, rather than Sagittarius and Capricorn shown here.

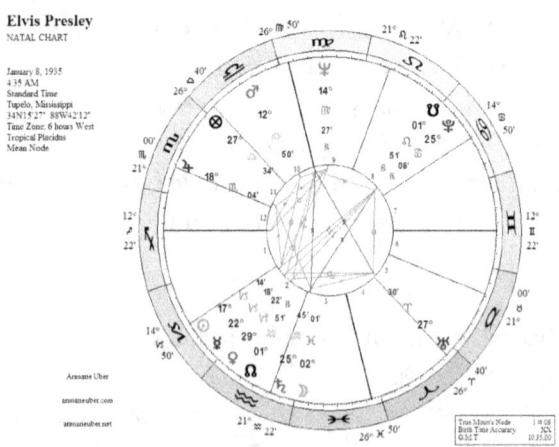

SIGNS OF A SOULMATE

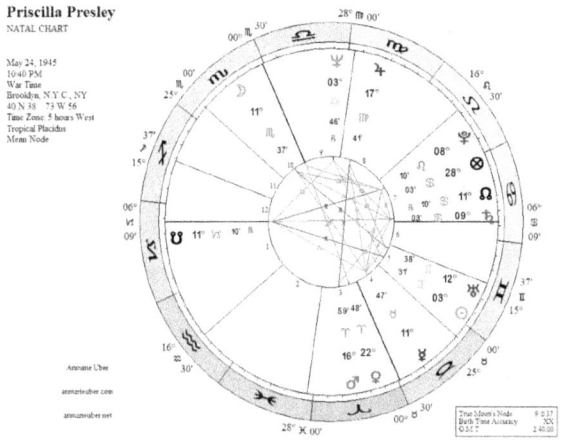

I also included Ann-Margaret's chart. Both Priscilla and Ann-Margaret scored around 5 or 6 with Elvis depending on which chart of Elvis' I used (there was a difference in the hand-drawn chart with his Moon sign). Is it any wonder Elvis was torn between these two women? If you read most media reports or listen to statements by those around Elvis at that time, they say Elvis was in love with Ann-Margaret but made a tough decision to stand by his word with Priscilla and marry her.

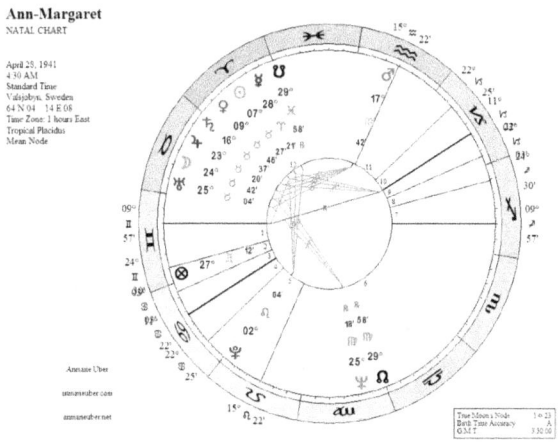

According to Priscilla:
"He was everything to me. My confidante, my husband, my everything."[7]

"I did not divorce him because I didn't love him. He was the love of my life, but I had to find out about the world."[8]

I thought it would be interesting to add the charts of Linda Thompson and Ginger Alden, the last two girlfriends of Elvis before he died. I didn't have a birth time for Ginger, but you can clearly see that she and Elvis loved each other and were engaged to be married. Note that their Sun signs were not in soulmate placements - meaning a soulmate is not dependent on having one of the Sun connections.

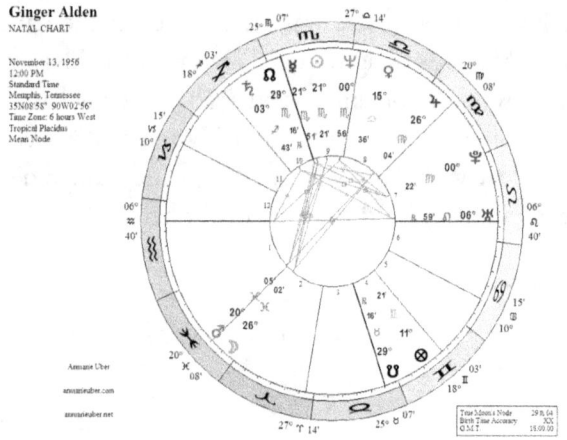

They have a Day Number connection of 4 and 8 and a connection with the Venus and Mars in Libra. Without a Sun connection (possibility of 2 – 3 points) or Ginger's birthtime to determine house connections *we don't know how high their score would be.*

. . .

Score: 2

Results: **Budding Romance**

2 – 4 Connections: Even though on the lower end of the scale, it is certainly a soulmate connection. You will need to work on possible differences for long-term harmony. This relationship can be more common to those shared with a friend or someone in your social circle. A Budding Romance may not create a tight enough bond for intimate relationships to go the distance, unless you are transparent with each other and have a clear intent to develop the relationship moving forward. This pairing has an energy of "getting to know each other and building something new" in this life but can be lasting if you are both emotionally mature and willing to work at it. You will have to protect the union from outside influences. There may also be a reason you came together that is not romantic – such as business or some other venture that would be more beneficial than romance.

In multiple interviews both Ann Margaret and Ginger Alden said they thought Elvis was their soulmate.

Here is Ginger telling what Elvis said to her:
"On the day he proposed, he said: 'Ginger, I've been searching for love so long, and never in my wildest dreams did I ever think I would find it in my own backyard. I've been 60% happy and 40% happy, but never 100%. I've loved before but I've never been in love. Ginger, I'm asking you, will you marry me?' Elvis brought his hand out from around his back. In it was a small, green velvet box. Nearly overcome by emotion, my voice quavered. 'Yes,' I managed. Our relationship had been so intense, as if he wanted me to know almost everything about him in a short time. I felt I'd found my soulmate. My hand was shaking as we kissed and stepped out of the bathroom into the bedroom. My hand was still trembling as he kept lifting it to look at the ring saying, 'oh boy.'"[9]

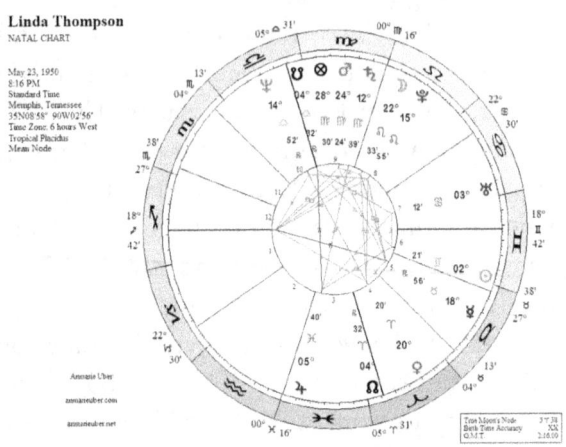

There are a lot of soulmate placements between Linda and Elvis:
Score: 8
Results: **Positive Friction**

8 - 10 Connections: This is an amazingly strong and beautiful connection. There is a lot of admiration and appreciation on both sides. Like two magnets drawn together, it was next to impossible that you wouldn't find each other in this lifetime. You feel supported and meet on common ground. The feeling is that you "know" the other person and have been together before. Probably through many lifetimes. There should be minimal conflict, but as every situation is unique this is not a hard fast rule. Issues could come up if each party is not in the place they need to be, to have a functional relationship. In that case, nurture strong communication skills and focus on your similarities, working through any difficult times with understanding and determination. It will be worth it in the long run, because you both can definitely be there for the long haul.

This quote from Linda sums up their charts and their scores:[10]

"Ours was a complete relationship—when the need arose, we got

to be everything to each other. He was almost sixteen years older than I and so it was natural for me to sometimes be the little girl, with him playing the daddy. More often than not, though, I was the mommy, and he was the baby. Sometimes we were lovers, sometimes we were brother and sister. Sometimes we were best friends. We were all things to each other at one time or another. And Elvis was always, always everything to me."

A CELEBRITY COUPLE WITH NO KNOWN BIRTH TIME

Kevin Bacon & Kyra Sedgwick

This couple does not have birth times on public record. I ran both charts at 12 noon (remember you can get a rectification chart done to figure out the probable time of birth) and skipped the questions in the quiz that pertained to house placements. They have been married since 1988. Let's see how they did with what we know.

ANMARIE UBER

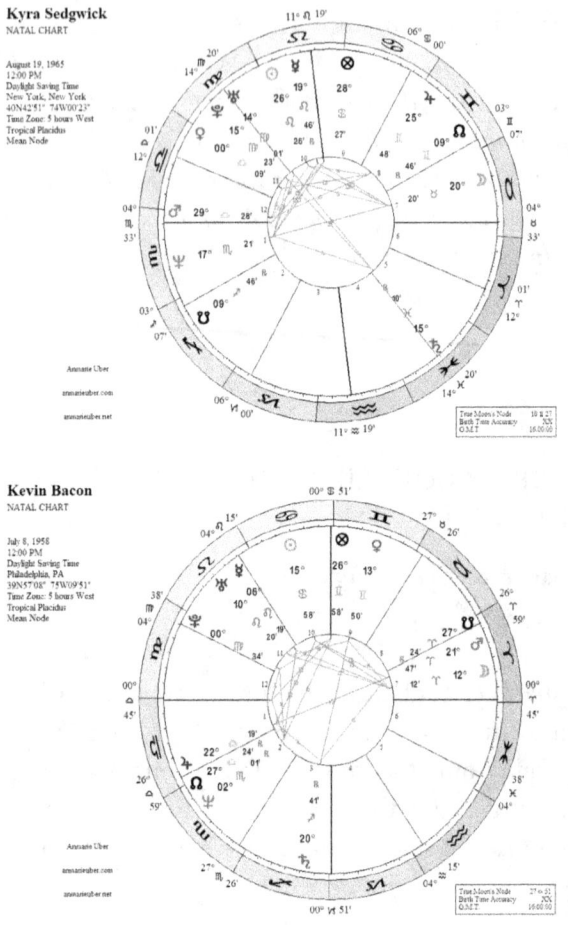

Score: 5

Results:

Note that they are scoring *at least* five, although knowing the house placements could have raised their points. However, I suspect these two have more placements than shown here, for as happy as they seem to be and how long they have stayed together.

Shooting Star

5 – 7 Connections: A great score that defines true soulmates. The two of you met and there were stars in your eyes ever since. This partnership has the potential to be long-lasting, although like

any relationship you will have to work on occasional difficulties or challenges and embrace your differences to keep the spark alive. But with this many points it is worth the effort to try. An astrology "synastry chart" can show additional harmonious factors – aspects between the planets and placements that increase compatibility and help solidify your bond. However, with a lot of difficult aspects or conflicting placements this could be a shooting star that aims high, burns hot and bright but could just as quickly burn out.

On their 27th anniversary, Kevin posted on Instagram:
"Celebrating 9,855 days of marriage to @kyrasedgwick."

It is also interesting to note that a 1 (Kyra) can be very lucky for an 8 (Kevin).

Afterword

Remember that all relationships between two people have value. Some are painful learning lessons that we need to leave behind and others have the potential to be something amazing. It is always the choice of both parties to stay together or part ways and many times couples who have high scores break up. This decision could be influenced by outside forces or any number of other factors. But usually, a breakup between linked soulmates is due to unresolved issues in one or both that make the relationship toxic, no matter how great the compatibility. So, have hope in love and remember it always begins with yourself.

I want to thank you so much for taking this journey with me and exploring connections between lovers from past lives. It has been my pleasure to log the patterns and write this book so that I could share it with you.

Much Love to You in this life.

We all deserve it.

If you enjoyed this book, please consider leaving a review.

Appendix

Quick Reference:

- Aries – Cardinal, Fire, 1ˢᵗ House, Mars ~ opposite Libra, Cardinal, 7ᵗʰ House, Venus

- Taurus – Fixed, Earth, 2ⁿᵈ House, Venus ~ opposite Scorpio, Fixed, 8ᵗʰ House, Pluto

- Gemini – Mutable, Air, 3ʳᵈ House, Mercury ~ opposite Sagittarius, Mutable, 9ᵗʰ House, Jupiter

- Cancer – Cardinal, Water, 4ᵗʰ House, Moon ~ opposite Capricorn, Cardinal, 10ᵗʰ House, Saturn

- Leo – Fixed, Fire, 5ᵗʰ House, Sun ~ opposite Aquarius, Fixed, 11ᵗʰ House, Uranus

- Virgo – Mutable, Earth, 6ᵗʰ House, Mercury ~ opposite Pisces, Mutable, 12ᵗʰ House, Neptune

Notes

3. THE 12 SIGNS OF VALENTINES

1. Soulmate Poetry, Uber, Anmarie, 2018
2. Walker, John Jacob, 1995
3. Soulmate Poetry, Uber, Anmarie, 2018, "Alchemy".
4. Soulmate Poetry, Uber, Anmarie 2018.
5. Soulmate Poetry, Uber, Anmarie, 2018, "Hidden Leo".
6. Soulmate Poetry, Uber, Anmarie, 2018 excerpt from "Virgo".
7. Soulmate Poetry, Uber, Anmarie, 2018, "Tristan"
8. Soulmate Poetry, Uber, Anmarie, 2018, "Scorpio to Scorpio".
9. Soulmate Poetry, Uber, Anmarie, 2018 excerpt.
10. Soulmate Poetry, Uber, Anmarie, 2018, "Lily Pad Limbo Land".
11. Soulmate Poetry, Uber, Anmarie, 2018, "Meeting My Match".
12. Soulmate Poetry, Uber, Anmarie, 2018, "A Frog is Always a Prince in Disguise" excerpt.

11. WRITTEN IN THE STARS - FAMOUS COUPLES

1. Today.com, Hines, Ree, May 5, 2017.
2. Today.com, Weisholtz, Drew, Oct. 6, 2020.
3. TheList.com, Mastrangelo, Fiama, Nov. 21, 2021.
4. Rollingout.com, Shropshire, Terry, Jan. 2, 2018 "Will Smith's beautiful 20-year wedding anniversary testimony to wife Jada."
5. Yahoo Entertainment, Aug. 2, 2013, "Sarah Michelle Gellar on 10-Year Freddie Prinze Jr. Marriage: "It's Work!"
6. People.com, Gliatto, Tom, Aug. 15, 1994, "Neverland Meets Graceland".
7. Closerweekly.com, Braun, Kelly, Jan. 12, 2020, "Elvis Presley and Priscilla Presley Are One of Hollywood's Most Iconic Couples! See Their Relationship Timeline".
8. Apost.com, apost team, March 26, 2021, "We reached for Tissues
9. Express News by Stefan Kyriazis, Thu, Aug 12, 2021 "Elvis' Final Days: Fiancée Ginger Describes their Heartbreaking Last Conversation".
10. News 35, March 6, 2021

About the Author

Anmarie Uber's interest in the metaphysical field has continued, throughout most of her life. She had her first remembered contact with the other side, at age three, and an insatiable passion throughout childhood to explore ghosts, UFOs and anything paranormal. She became interested in astrology and numerology which led to studying tarot, yoga, massage, nutrition, palmistry, crystal healing, Feng Shui, energy healing, and the philosophy of reincarnation by age 21. Her ongoing quest for spiritual truth has been all-consuming, and has many times taken precedence over having a personal life or worldly goals. What she has found is that many "new age" and other belief systems can be roads to nowhere...another program to be sifted through. Although Anmarie has studied and lived countless spiritual and religious ideologies, the last five years of her life have been the most challenging as the pressure to keep humanity down is increasing. Anmarie believes in finding the humor in difficult situations to keep hold of your sanity and in trusting in your own inner voice that knows the truth. She believes we are all programmed beings trying to awaken from a mass hypnosis...and awakening to your true Self and finding the answers to who you are, where you are, why you are here and where you are going after is the most important accomplishment you can achieve in life.

www.ingramcontent.com/pod-product-compliance
Lightning Source LLC
Chambersburg PA
CBHW070544010526
44118CB00012B/1208